# Dramascripts

# The Canterbury Tales

**A play based on the poem by Geoffrey Chaucer**

John O'Connor

Published in 2001 by:
Nelson Thornes Ltd
Delta Place
27 Bath Road
CHELTENHAM
GL53 7TH
United Kingdom

08 / 10 9 8 7 6 5 4

A catalogue record for this book is available from the British Library

ISBN 978 0 17 432658 8

Illustrations by Zhenya Matysiak
Page make-up by Peter Nickol

Printed and bound in Croatia by Zrinski

# CONTENTS

# Series Editor's Introduction

Dramascripts is an exciting series of plays especially chosen for students in lower and middle years of secondary school. The titles range from the best in modern writing to adaptations of classic texts such as *A Christmas Carol* and *Silas Marner*.

Dramascripts can be read or acted purely for the enjoyment and stimulation that they provide; however, each play in the series also offers all the support that pupils need in working with the text in the classroom:

- **Introduction** – this offers important background information and explains something about the ways in which the play came to be written.
- **Script** – this is clearly set out in ways that make the play easy to handle in the classroom.
- **Notes** explain references that pupils might not understand, and language points that are not obvious.
- **Activities** – at the end of scenes, acts or sections – give pupils the opportunity to explore the play more fully. Types of activity include: discussion, writing, hot-seating, improvisation, acting, freeze-framing, story-boarding and artwork.
- **Looking Back at the Play** – this section has further activities for more extended work on the play as a whole, with emphasis on characters, plots, themes and language.

*John O'Connor*

# Introduction:
## *The Canterbury Tales*

### GEOFFREY CHAUCER

Geoffrey Chaucer was born some time around 1340 in London. As a young man, he fought in the wars between England and France and was taken prisoner, but the King paid a ransom to get him back. After that he became a diplomat, travelling to France and Italy on missions for the King. It was possibly while he was abroad that he read books by the famous Italian

writers Dante, Petrarch and Boccaccio, whose stories he later used as some of the *Canterbury Tales*. In 1374 he was made Controller of Customs in the Port of London, but by this time he had begun a career as a writer which was to make him famous. His best known works are *The Parliament of Fowls*, *The Canterbury Tales* and *Troilus and Criseyde*, a tragic love story set in the Trojan war.

Chaucer became a Member of Parliament in his late forties, and was then given the post of Clerk of the King's Works, which involved looking after the royal estates. He died in 1400 and is buried in Westminster Abbey.

## CANTERBURY AND PILGRIMAGES

*The Canterbury Tales* is Chaucer's most famous work. It begins in the springtime when a group of about thirty travellers have met to embark on a pilgrimage to Canterbury. Pilgrimages were very popular in Chaucer's time. People would journey together to some sacred place which was important for their religious faith. Canterbury was the most popular centre for pilgrims in England, because it was the cathedral in which Thomas Becket, Henry II's Archbishop, had been assassinated two centuries earlier. Many people visited Becket's tomb believing that the martyr (now made a saint) could cure them of sickness.

## CHAUCER'S *CANTERBURY TALES*

When Chaucer wrote *The Canterbury Tales*, he made himself part of the group of pilgrims, and he starts off by describing them to us, one by one. (In this play version, that job is done by the Host of the inn and his assistant.)

Chaucer wrote in a language which we now call Middle English. The language has changed a good deal in the six hundred years and more since Chaucer was alive. But, as you will see, his stories still have the power to make us laugh, to give us food for thought and even to make our flesh creep.

# The Characters

Based at Southwark:
The **HOST**, or landlord of the Tabard Inn, Harry Bailey
**WILLIAM**, his assistant manager

The pilgrims:
The **MILLER**, Robin; a huge, powerful man with a wart on his nose
The **COOK**, Hodge of Ware; skilful if unhygienic
The **WIFE OF BATH**, an attractive woman in her fifties who has had five husbands
The **KNIGHT**, a military man in a battle-stained tunic
The **SQUIRE**, the Knight's brightly dressed son of twenty
The **FRANKLIN**, a good-natured, white-bearded land-owner in his sixties
The **SCHOLAR**, an underfed Oxford student
**GEOFFREY CHAUCER**, a writer and civil servant in his mid-forties
The **PRIORESS**, Madam Eglentyne; attractive, elegant and expensively dressed
The **MONK**, bald, well-fed, well-off and fond of hunting
The **FRIAR**, Hubert; a great visitor of inns and women
The **SUMMONER**, a spotty, pimply fines-collector
The **PARDONER**, the summoner's friend; thin, with long blond hair and
    a high voice
The **PARSON**, poor, honest and generous
The **PLOUGHMAN**, the parson's brother, and a similar character
The **REEVE**, Oswald; a skinny and bad-tempered carpenter from Norfolk
The **SHIPMAN**, from Dartmouth; a tanned and experienced navigator
The **MANCIPLE**, a clever college caterer
The **DOCTOR**, a physician made rich by the plague
The **LAWYER**, knowledgeable, busy and at the top of his profession
The **MERCHANT**, a wealthy cross-channel trader
The **NUN**, young and idealistic

plus: **MARY** and **JEAN**, on their way back from Canterbury

also, at Boughton: **A GULLIBLE VILLAGER**

---

Characters in *The Pardoner's Tale*:
**SIDNEY DELMAR**, a small-time London crook of the 1950s
**MAVIS**, his girl
**JOHNNIE**, **RONALD** and **CYRIL**, three members of Delmar's gang
**ERIC**, a nervous gang-member
The **MATCH-SELLER**
The **SHOPKEEPER**

Characters in *The Reeves's Tale*:
A **MILLER**
The **MILLER'S WIFE** and **DAUGHTER**
**ALAN** and **JOHN**, students

Characters in *Chaucer's Tale of Sir Topaze*:
**SIR TOPAZE**, short and fat, mid-thirties
His **MUM** and **DAD**
A **POSTMAN** (doubling as) an **UMPIRE**
A **BOWLER**, impressive, wearing West Indies colours

Characters in *The Franklin's Tale*:
**GUS**, a major, mid-thirties
**DORRIE**, his wife, the same age
**PETER**, a young lieutenant
A **FAKIR**, an Indian holy man
A **SOLDIER**
The **BRIGADIER'S WIFE**, mid-fifties and powerful
**MRS JOPLIN** and **MILDRED**, officers' wives

Characters in *The Miller's Tale*:
**JEAN-PIERRE**, fifty, a café-owner
**ALICE**, his young and attractive wife
**NICOLAS**, their young lodger; an artist in love with Alice
**ABSALON**, the local curate, also in love with Alice

The play was originally written for, and performed by, the people of Wheatley, Oxfordshire, with music composed by Roger Simmonds. It has since been performed at the Oxford Playhouse.

# THE CANTERBURY TALES
## SCENE 1

*The Tabard Inn, Southwark. April 1385*

*Enter the HOST, Harry Bailey.*

**HOST**      Welcome! My name's Harry Bailey and this is The Tabard. If    **1**
you're looking for a soft bed, hot food and the best beer this
side of the Thames, you've come to the right place. For those
of you who haven't found it yet, Southwark Cathedral's
down Pig Lane and turn left.

*Whispered approval from the PRIORESS'S ENTOURAGE.*

And the bar's through there and turn right.

*The MILLER and COOK set off.*

Opening time after supper!

*MILLER and COOK return, grumbling.*    **10**

We're seriously short-handed in the bar, sad to say, it being
Spring Bank Holiday. Oh, and another thing. We're a trifle
over-booked, but I'm sure you won't mind sharing.

*Varying reactions, including:*

**WIFE OF BATH**      I booked a single room.

**HOST**      Complain to your travel agent. Now, my man will arrange for

**tabard** *a sleeveless top-coat which a knight wore over his armour.*

**Southwark** *now part of London, on the south bank of the Thames.*

your bags to be taken up. Supper will be served in about ten minutes.

*Over the ensuing hubbub, he calls:*

William!

*WILLIAM comes running.*

| | |
|---|---|
| **WILLIAM** | Guvnor? |
| **HOST** | Is this the lot? |
| **WILLIAM** | Pretty well. We had a cancellation from a dodgy Canon's Yeoman. |
| **HOST** | I'll contain my disappointment. Where are they stowed? |
| **WILLIAM** | Well… |

*As he reads from his list, lighting picks out the relevant groups. Some are chatting, some unpacking upstairs. At the same time, SERVANTS bustle around, collecting the remaining pilgrims' luggage and taking them off to their rooms.*

I put the Knight and his Squire upstairs in the posh room. Next door to them we've got the Franklin, plus an Oxford scholar and a Mr Chalker…

| | |
|---|---|
| **HOST** | That's Chaucer. |
| **WILLIAM** | *(Pencilling in a correction.)* Right. |
| **HOST** | What about the Prioress? Looks a bit fussy. |
| **WILLIAM** | She's in the annexe. |

**canon's yeoman** *an assistant to a priest; in Chaucer's poem, he joins the pilgrimage late.*

**franklin** *a well-off land-owner.*

**prioress** *a woman in charge of nuns in a convent.*

**annexe** *extension to the main building.*

| | |
|---|---|
| **HOST** | Fine. |
| **WILLIAM** | Sharing with the woman from Bath. |
| **HOST** | Are you serious? Not the whinger with the big hat? |
| **WILLIAM** | Problem? |
| **HOST** | Not so long as they're both prepared to broaden their experience a bit. |
| **WILLIAM** | This is a pilgrimage, guvnor. |
| **HOST** | Fair point. Go on. |
| **WILLIAM** | And we've got all the clerical gentlemen in the long dorm. |
| **HOST** | Usual collection? |
| **WILLIAM** | *(Nods.)* Run of the mill: one Monk – over there, stuffing his face. A Friar next to him – watch the women. Oh, and the ugly one's a Summoner, eats garlic. And the blond… |
| **HOST** | Is a Pardoner. Yes, we've met. He tried to sell me a bone from Saint Peter's finger this morning. |
| **WILLIAM** | I trust you didn't purchase, guvnor. |
| **HOST** | I did not. I merely observed that Saint Peter missed his vocation as a harpist. He's got thirty-seven fingers that I know of. Carry on. |
| **WILLIAM** | The Parson and Ploughman are brothers – by themselves |

40

50

**clerical** *belonging to the church.*

**summoner** *a church official whose job it was to issue summonses and fines to people who broke religious rules, such as not going to church; summoners were notorious for taking bribes and pocketing the fines.*

**pardoner** *a man who sold 'pardons': people paid money to be let off their sins; many (perhaps most) pardoners were frauds and con-men.*

over there. I put them downstairs with the skinny Carpenter – moonlights as a Reeve, apparently. Plus a seafaring man from Dartmouth; and a college caterer…

**HOST**    Manciple.

*As WILLIAM grudgingly repeats 'Manciple' and corrects it on his list, HARRY looks over his shoulder and asks:*

Who are 'Robin' and 'Hodge of Ware'?

**WILLIAM**    A Miller and a Cook. At present they are harmessly engaged in exchanging filthy stories. When they arrived they were as tight as owls. So they're dossing down tonight in the stable.

**HOST**    Very prudent. Hang on, according to my list, we've also got a Doctor, a Lawyer and a Merchant. Where are they?

**WILLIAM**    Up on the balcony. Discussing the Stock Market, I should imagine.

**HOST**    I mean, where are they sleeping? You've not put them in the stable, have you?

**WILLIAM**    Don't be daft, guvnor.

**HOST**    That's a relief.

**WILLIAM**    They're in your room.

*Before we can register HARRY's reaction, a number of conversations arise, snippets of which are picked out like a kind of sound collage, again assisted by spotlighting.*

**WIFE OF BATH**    *(To the PRIORESS.)* …Bath. Well, just outside actually. My first three husbands left me very well provided for. Just as

**reeve** *an official on an estate, who collected the money which was to be paid to the lord of the manor.*

**manciple** *somebody who bought the provisions for a large institution such as a college.*

well; the fourth was uncontrollable – you know what men
are like… *(Gaffe!)* Sorry…

**DOCTOR**   *(To the MERCHANT and LAWYER.)* …no, it's like any of the
caring professions, really. You get a lean year… then along
comes a filthy hot summer, a nice little dose of the Black
Death, and you're back in business… *(Laughs.)*

**MILLER**   *(To the COOK.)* …So he marries this really young girl, right?
Young enough to be his daughter…

**KNIGHT**   *(To the SQUIRE, who is unbuckling him.)* …no time to change,
young 'un. Back from Crusades. Disembark Dover;
rendezvous Southwark 0800 hours… *(Thinks.)* Could have

90

gone straight to Canterbury, come to think of it…

**CHAUCER**  (*To the FRANKLIN.*) …no, no. For a long time I was in the Civil Service. Writing was a bit of a pastime, really.

**FRANKLIN**  (*Laughing.*) Well, just so long as you're not planning to put any of us in your books, eh?

*They laugh together, the FRANKLIN more wholeheartedly than CHAUCER.*

*Music.*

*The last of the pilgrims disappear, led off by servants to their accommodation, leaving CHAUCER alone on stage. He takes a notebook out of his pocket and is about to write something down when WILLIAM enters to collect his bag and take him to his room. The lights change to signify the passage of day into night, then night into dawn, and the music ends with the cock crowing.*

**WRITING** Draw up three columns. In the first, list the pilgrims. You might call them by their job or title (for example, the Franklin), their name, or, in some cases, both. In the second column make a note of who they share a room with in the Tabard Inn. In the third column, add anything else that we know about them at this stage. Keep the chart and add to it as you learn more about the pilgrims. One entry might start off like this:

| Pilgrim | Rooming with | Other information |
|---|---|---|
| *a seafaring man* | *Parson, Ploughman, Carpenter (a Reeve)* | *He comes from Dartmouth* |

**PERFORMING** If you were planning to perform this opening scene, how would you stage it? Draw some sketches or plans and write notes to show how each group of characters might be shown to the audience as the Host and William discuss them.

**LANGUAGE STUDY**  This is how Chaucer himself described some of his pilgrims, when he wrote The Canterbury Tales in the fourteenth century. In pairs, work out a translation of each description, using the notes to help you. Then add some of the details to your pilgrim chart.

| | |
|---|---|
| the Knight | Of <u>fustian</u> he <u>wered</u> a <u>gypon</u>   (rough cloth; wore; tunic) |
| | Al <u>bismotered</u> with his <u>habergeoun</u>   (stained; chain mail) |
| the Squire | A <u>lovyere</u> and a <u>lusty bacheler</u>   (lover; vigorous trainee knight) |
| the Yeoman | And he was clad in cote and hood of grene. |
| the Prioress | And she was <u>cleped</u> Madame Eglentine   (called) |
| the Monk | His heed was <u>balled</u>, that shoon as any glas   (bald) |
| the Friar | He was the beste beggere in his <u>hous</u>   (friary) |
| the Merchant | A Marchant was ther with a forked berd |
| the Scholar | And leene was his hors as is a rake |
| the Lawyer | <u>Nowher</u> so busy a man as he <u>ther nas</u>   (there was not…anywhere) |
| | And yet he <u>semed</u> busier than he was.   (seemed) |
| the Franklin | Whit was his <u>berd</u> as is a <u>daiesye</u>   (beard; daisy) |
| the Cook | …on his shin a <u>mormel</u> hadde he   (ulcer) |
| the Doctor | He kepte <u>that he wan in pestilence</u>   (what he earned during the plague) |
| the Wife of Bath | Boold was hir face, and fair, and reed of <u>hewe</u>.   (complexion) |
| the Parson | He was also a lerned man, a <u>clerk</u>   (scholar) |
| the Ploughman | A <u>trewe swinkere</u> and a good was he   (honest labourer) |
| the Miller | Upon <u>the cope right</u> of his nose he hade   (the very tip) |
| | A <u>werte</u>, and theron stood a <u>toft of heris</u>   (wart; tuft of hairs) |
| | <u>Reed</u> as the <u>brustles</u> of a <u>sowes eris</u>.   (red; bristles; sows' ears) |
| the Reeve | The Reve was a <u>sclendre coleric</u> man   (thin, bad-tempered) |
| the Summoner | For <u>saucefleem</u> he was, with eyen <u>narwe</u>   (pimply; narrow) |
| the Pardoner | This pardoner hadde <u>heer</u> as yelow as <u>wex</u>   (hair; wax) |
| | …But thinne it lay, <u>by colpons, oon and oon</u>   (in rats' tails, one by one) |
| the Host | A <u>large</u> man he was with <u>eyen stepe</u>   (broad; bright eyes) |

Look carefully at Chaucer's descriptions of the pilgrims in the activity above. He wrote in a language we now call Middle English. How different does it seem to be from Modern English? Look at his vocabulary and make two lists: (i)  words in Chaucer's English which are no longer recognisable today (such as 'gypon' for tunic); and (ii) words which are only slightly different from their modern English versions (such as 'lovyere' for lover). Count up the totals for each list. Then (iii) do a rough count of the words which don't seem to have changed at all (such as 'of', 'he', 'with', 'his'…). When you look at your three totals, would you say that Chaucer's vocabulary was very different from yours, or generally similar?

# *SCENE 2*

*The Tabard Inn. The following morning.*

*Lights up as HARRY enters with CHAUCER, closely followed by a crowd of the other pilgrims.*

HOST

So let me get this straight. I get a free trip to Canterbury, all expenses covered; the condition being that I judge this story-telling contest, right?

*Encouraging noises from the CROWD.*

CHAUCER

Correct. And you provide a slap-up supper for the winner when we return.

HOST

Stuff that!

CHAUCER

All right, we'll have a whip-round to cover it.

HOST

You're on.

*General approving noises.*

When do we start?

CHAUCER

Whenever the horses are ready, I presume.

HOST

No, I mean, when do we start the stories? I calculate you're talking about thirty travellers, two tales there, two tales back, that's a hundred and twenty tales. Get a couple in now while they're loading up, or we've no chance of getting through them.

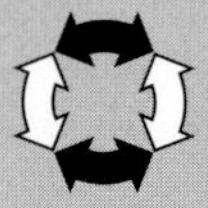

**DISCUSSION** In pairs, talk about the arrangement that the Host agrees to concerning the story-telling contest. If you had been on the pilgrimage, why might a contest like this have seemed a good idea?

*There is a pause as they acknowledge the sense of his argument.*

So who's first?

*Each one anxious to avoid the honour, there is an awkward murmur of people excusing themselves and helpfully suggesting other people. The sound is interrupted by the clear, and rather feminine, tones of the PARDONER. He clearly sees this as a marketing opportunity.*

# *The Pardoner's Tale*

**PARDONER**    Once upon a time…    1

*The on-stage PILGRIMS immediately form an audience, joined by others who have come down from their rooms, and by the SERVANTS. The only exceptions are the actors who are about to become the characters in the Pardoner's tale: these begin to don appropriate garments and collect props from the laundry baskets and remaining luggage.*

…there was a gang of ne'er-do-wells, whose lives were dedicated to the pursuit of gluttony, sloth, wrath, lechery and – particularly – avarice… the sin of greed…    10

*The pilgrims find spaces in which to make themselves comfortable. Meanwhile, we hear music: a dance band plays 'Money is the root of all evil'.*

**gluttony**… *Some of the Seven Deadly Sins: gluttony is eating too much; sloth is laziness; wrath is anger; lechery is sex; avarice (not officially one of the seven) is greed for money.*

*We are in the HQ of a small-time London gangster of the fifties, SIDNEY DELMAR. He is dressed as a spiv and reclines in an armchair (pushed in from off-stage), drinking beer from a bottle, smoking and reading the 'Sporting Life'. The music comes from a gramophone of the period.*

*His girl, MAVIS, a young teddy-girl, is jiving nearby to the music. Three henchmen are playing cards on an upturned box, smoking and drinking. Two of them, JOHNNIE and RONALD, are very sharp teddy-boys. The third, CYRIL, is a rather lumbering heavy. They are arguing ad lib about who owes what in their poker game.*

*Enter ERIC, a nervous side-kick, breathless. SYDNEY motions to MAVIS to lift the needle off the record and, as the music ends with an ugly scratching sound, the three henchmen notice the panting ERIC.*

| | |
|---|---|
| **DELMAR** | You look flustered, Eric. What's up? Don't tell me they're rationing sweeties again. |
| **ERIC** | This is serious, Mr Delmar. |
| **DELMAR** | Serious, he says. Well, come on then, Eric my son. Deliver. |
| **ERIC** | I've just been with the law, Mr Delmar. |
| **DELMAR** | You stun me, Eric. And? |
| **ERIC** | It's Loftie McLean, Mr Delmar. He's dead. |

*Silence. JOHNNIE stands.*

| | |
|---|---|
| **DELMAR** | First Lennie. Then Harold the Fence. Yesterday the Parker twins. Now Lofty. *(To himself.)* Who, who, who? |

**rationing** *after the Second World War, items such as sweets were rationed: you could only buy a certain amount each week.*

**fence** *someone who accepts stolen goods.*

| | | |
|---|---|---|
| **ERIC** | Nobody knows, Mr Delmar. The law, his gang. Nobody knows. | |
| **DELMAR** | Well somebody did for him. | 40 |
| **ERIC** | Or something, Mr Delmar. | |
| **DELMAR** | Something? Something? Something like what? A number eleven bus? A British Railways sandwich? Boris Karloff? | |
| **ERIC** | I don't know, Mr Delmar. He was found with a knife in his back down Hammersmith tube station… The Piccadilly Line… | |
| **DELMAR** | As the lady said, Eric, the line is immaterial. | |
| **ERIC** | Sorry, Mr Delmar. | |
| **DELMAR** | The knife, sadly, is not. | |
| **ERIC** | I know. And all the boys are saying it's a bit funny, like. I mean, what with five of the gang going so sudden and mysterious. | 50 |
| **DELMAR** | There's nothing funny about it. This isn't the Curse of the Mummy's Tomb. Your little imagination's running away with you, Eric. I can see I'm going to have to confiscate your ABC Minors badge. | |
| | *ERIC's hand goes protectively to his lapel.* | |
| **JOHNNIE** | But he's got something, Mr Delmar. It's not just our boys – the Fulham Road mob's been done an' all – four of 'em. | |
| **DELMAR** | I am aware of that, Johnnie. I'm just saying there's nothing spooky about it. | 60 |

**Boris Karloff** *the actor who played Frankenstein's monster in a famous film version.*

**ABC Minors** *a cinema club for children.*

| | |
|---|---|
| **JOHNNIE** | Well, who did for 'em, then? |
| **DELMAR** | That, Johnnie, is what we – or, to be more accurate, you – are going to find out. Somebody is systematically taking out all the big names from Walham Green to Hammersmith Broadway. If he makes his way to Shepherd's Bush, we're in dead trouble, my son. |
| **JOHNNIE** | What do we do, Mr Delmar? |
| **DELMAR** | Well, for number one, we don't just sit here like the three little pigs waiting to be gobbled up. |
| **CYRIL** | *(After some laborious counting.)* Four little pigs, Mr Delmar. |
| **DELMAR** | *(Studiously ignoring him.)* We go out. We look. We ask. |
| **JOHNNIE** | Where, though? |
| **DELMAR** | Well, I suppose you could try the Women's Institute. I hear the Kensington Ladies Flower-arranging Circle's got some pretty dodgy customers we might learn a thing or two from. |
| **RONALD** | Are they a new mob, Mr Delmar? |
| **DELMAR** | Use your loaf, Ronald. I'll lay you any odds you like this isn't anybody we know. Ask about strangers. Look for strangers. Question strangers, Ronald. You know the way. |
| **RONALD** | Right, Mr Delmar. |
| **DELMAR** | Meanwhile I'll see what I can pick up on the grapevine tonight. |
| | *DELMAR collects MAVIS's fur and gestures her to follow him.* |
| **RONALD** | Where's he going tonight? |
| **JOHNNIE** | It's Thursday, remember. |
| **RONALD** | Oh, yeh. |
| **CYRIL** | What's Thursday? |

| | |
|---|---|
| **JOHNNIE** | Freemasons. |

*Music: 'Money is the root of all evil' fades quickly up and then down* **90** *as the chair and gramophone are removed. As the music disappears, we hear the sound of a street market. Every minute or so an underground train passes.*

**JOHNNIE**   …fell off the back of a lorry, they told him.

**RONALD**   He said they was Italian too.

*CYRIL has seen someone in the crowd. He tries to interrupt.*

We got time for a cup of Bovril, Johnnie? My plates are killing me. I think it's these new crepes.

*CYRIL tries again.*

**JOHNNIE**   Sorry, Ron, my son – no time; we're working, remember – **100** hang on, Cyril – and the boss is not going to be best pleased – in a minute, Cyril – if we go back tonight – if you can't wait, go over there behind the soft fruits – without – Cyril, what is it?

**CYRIL**   By the papers, Johnnie. He's a stranger, isn't he?

*He indicates an old MATCH-SELLER standing in the corner.*

**JOHNNIE**   Well, he's strange. I'll give him that.

**RONALD**   Just some old blind man, John. He can't tell us anything.

**JOHNNIE**   We try everybody new, Ronald. Come on.

*They approach the old man menacingly.* **110**

**Freemasons**  *a secret society, mainly for businessmen.*

**plates**  *cockney rhyming slang: 'plates o' meat' (= feet).*

**crepes**  *soft-soled shoes.*

| | |
|---|---|
| **MATCH-SELLER** | Matches… matches… You want some matches, sir? |
| **JOHNNIE** | Got any Swan Vestas? *(The MATCH-SELLER obliges.)* |
| **MATCH-SELLER** | Anything else? |
| **JOHNNIE** | Yes. Information. |
| **MATCH-SELLER** | What about? |
| **JOHNNIE** | I think you know what about. |
| **MATCH-SELLER** | I'm only an old blind foreigner. What can I tell you? |
| **RONALD** | Wednesday night. |
| **JOHNNIE** | A death. |
| **MATCH-SELLER** | Death. Ah. |

*The old man examines JOHNNIE's face with his hands. JOHNNIE becomes frightened and grabs the man's wrists.*

| | |
|---|---|
| **JOHNNIE** | You know something, don't you? I can tell. *(The old man remains silent.)* I said you know. *(He grabs the man's lapels.)* You know what we're talking about. You know how they died. You're part of it. |
| **RONALD** | Leave him, Johnnie, leave him alone. He's just some crazy old git. Leave him. |
| **JOHNNIE** | Well, are you? Is that all you are? |

*Silence. A train passes overhead.*

| | |
|---|---|
| **MATCH-SELLER** | There is a music shop. Closed down now. Bomb hit it in the war. Through the railway arches by the bookstall. |
| **JOHNNIE** | I know the place. |

**Swan Vestas** *an old brand of matches.*

| RONALD | *(Looking over his shoulder.)* Johnnie, the rozzers! |
|---|---|
| JOHNNIE | We'll go there. But I'm warning you – if we don't find anything – |
| | *They go quickly.* |
| MATCH-SELLER | You'll find something. |

**DISCUSSION** In pairs talk about what you think is going to happen. Remember that the three men have gone out to find a killer; and that the match-seller – whom they haven't seen in the market before – tells them mysteriously 'You'll find something'. What will they find, do you think? How will it affect them?

**PERFORMING** Prepare a short performance of the scene in the market (from '...fell off the back of a lorry' to 'You'll find something'). First of all, think about the characters. For example, the match-seller could be a sinister figure. What should he look like? How should he speak? Try to contrast the 'tough' behaviour of the three men with the more thoughtful speech of the match-seller.

| | *The noise of the market builds up, then fades into music: Frankie Vaughan's 'Green Door'.* |
|---|---|
| | *As the music fades, we are in an old disused shop, represented by boxes and crates littering the floor. The three men are ransacking it, throwing old newspapers around, breaking open crates.* |
| RONALD | Nothing! I'm for going back and doing that old git right now. |
| JOHNNIE | But he knew something, Ron. He knew what we were talking about. And I'll lay a tenner he knows who killed the boys. |

140

**rozzers** *slang term for the police.*

**I'll lay a tenner** *I'll bet ten pounds.*

*CYRIL has been scrutinising a newspaper, picked up from the floor. He reads painfully:*

**CYRIL**    'Scunthorpe man wins a quarter of a million. It will not change my life in any way, he says…'

**JOHNNIE**    It'd sure enough change my life, I can tell you…

*RONALD sits and lights a cigarette, offers one to JOHNNIE, who accepts and finds a box to sit on away from the others.*

Women… cars… booze… South of France… (*Unable to shift the box he wants to sit on, he kicks at it angrily.*) Christ! What's in this? 'Ere, get it open, Cyril. (*CYRIL forces the lid with a crowbar.*) I've had enough of this game, Ron. I'm not kidding, I'm on the point of turning straight, I don't mind admitting it.

*He is interrupted by a wild babbling sound from CYRIL, who is staring at the contents of the chest.*

For Christ's sake, Cyril…

**RONALD**    (*Who has joined CYRIL and is looking into the chest.*) Johnnie. Come here.

*JOHNNIE goes across to the others and looks in. There is a brief silence. Then uncontrolled and extremely noisy ecstasy, including snatches of the words 'rich' and 'gold'. Finally they subside sufficiently to be intelligible.*

**JOHNNIE**    Cyril, we are rich, my son – what do they say? – beyond our wildest imaginings.

**RONALD**    Of course! The Isleworth Provincial Bank job. There was gold in that; but they never said how much.

**JOHNNIE**    Come off it, Ron. The McLeans did Isleworth with the Fulham boys. They're not in this league.

**CYRIL**    Maybe they didn't know what they was nicking – I never do.

| | |
|---|---|
| **RONALD** | Cyril, for once, in your simple-minded way, you might have hit it. |
| **CYRIL** | *(Pleased.)* Thanks, Ron. |
| **JOHNNIE** | We've got to get it out. Get it back to the flat. |
| **RONALD** | How? It weighs a ton. |
| **CYRIL** | What about a pram? |
| **RONALD** | In broad daylight? Through Shepherd's Bush market? |
| **JOHNNIE** | All right. One of us goes out, right? Picks up half a dozen good stout beer crates, brings 'em back here. We hole out til tomorrow morning and then nip out while they're delivering for the market. Nobody'll take any notice of us. |
| **RONALD** | All right. Who goes, who stays? |
| **JOHNNIE** | *(Producing a pack of cards.)* Lowest card goes. All right? |
| **RONALD** | Suppose so. Cyril can go first. |
| **CYRIL** | Suits me. *(Cuts.)* Ten of clubs. |
| **RONALD** | Johnnie? |
| **JOHNNIE** | Don't you trust me, Ron? *(Cuts)* Seven of hearts. |

*RONALD cuts and looks at his card. JOHNNIE turns RON's hand to see what it is.*

Six of hearts. Good job there wasn't much at stake, eh, Ronald? *(RONALD doesn't reply.)* Right. Off you go then, my son. And see if you can pick up some drink and a bit o' nosh. Couple or three quarts o' pig's ear'll go down very nicely after a good day's work.

*RONALD nods curtly and goes.*

---

**pig's ear** *cockney rhyming slang (= beer).*

---

| | |
|---|---|
| **JOHNNIE** | *(Laughs and reclines in an old chair.)* Rich beyond our wildest imaginings! |

*CYRIL has been fiddling with an old gramophone and some records. It suddenly strikes up with 'Money is the root of all evil'.*

*CYRIL begins a clumsy dance to the music. JOHNNIE laughs throughout as he reclines and smokes. The effect is sinister.*

**JOHNNIE**   *(As the music ends.)* What else you got, Cyril?

**CYRIL**   *(Reads.)* 'Tea for Two. Victor Sylvester and the BBC Dance Orchestra.'

**JOHNNIE**   *(The serious thought which has been at the back of his mind surfaces, and he sits up.)* Tea for two.

**CYRIL**   Want it?

**JOHNNIE**   What?

**CYRIL**   'Tea for Two'.

**JOHNNIE**   Sit down, Cyril. How long we been partners? Can't be far off twenty years.

**CYRIL**   Since we left Ladbroke Secondary.

**JOHNNIE**   Long time. *(Pause.)* You never did like the idea of Ron joining us, did you? You're not what you'd call mates exactly, are you?

**CYRIL**   He's all right. Takes the mickey a bit.

**JOHNNIE**   *(Nods sympathetically.)* 'Course, it could be just you and me again. Like in the old days, Cyril. *(Looks at him.)* Tea for two, eh?

*The lights dim on the main stage and come up on one of the higher levels, where RONALD is buying something from a depressing-looking shopkeeper.*

**SHOPKEEPER**   Rats?

**RONALD**   Yeh, rats. I live down the canal, right?

| | |
|---|---|
| **SHOPKEEPER** | Sure. So you want to kill some rats. |
| **RONALD** | Right. |
| **SHOPKEEPER** | Cost you. |
| **RONALD** | How much? |
| **SHOPKEEPER** | A pony to you. |
| | *RON nods and the transaction is completed.* |
| **RONALD** | Er, how much do I…? |
| **SHOPKEEPER** | *(Smiles.)* Just a drop. And it's quite tasteless. |

*As the SHOPKEEPER pockets the money he calls after RON, who has descended to a lower level.*

240

Be careful what you do with the bodies!

| | |
|---|---|
| **RONALD** | *(Terrified.)* What? |
| **SHOPKEEPER** | Rats. They carry nasty diseases. |

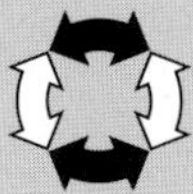

**DISCUSSION**  Now predict in pairs how you think the story will end. Think about the plan that Johnnie and Cyril have discussed (why does Johnnie stress the title of the song 'Tea for Two'?), and Ronald's visit to the poison-seller. Try to work out exactly what will happen when Ronald gets back to the others.

**a pony**  *slang for twenty-five pounds.*

*RON nods again and goes. But he stays on the raised level. Checking that he is not being observed, he takes three bottles of beer from his bag, puts one in his pocket and proceeds to add poison to the other two. As he does so, he begins to sing 'Tea for Two' in a macabre fashion. As he completes his preparation of the bottles, we hear the recorded version merging with his voice.*

*Music: 'Tea for Two'. Lights up on the shop. JOHNNIE and CYRIL are ballroom-dancing to the record. RONALD enters, taps JOHNNIE on the shoulder, as though in an 'excuse-me', and begins to dance with CYRIL. JOHNNIE laughs and stands to one side. He opens his flick-knife and taps RONALD on the shoulder. RONALD turns and, as he smilingly takes JOHNNIE in a ballroom-hold, JOHNNIE stabs him.*

*As JOHNNIE cleans his knife, CYRIL gets the bottles out of RONALD's bag. After a mimed 'cheers', they drink. The poison takes effect quickly and dramatically.*

*As they crumple to the floor next to the lifeless RONALD, the music comes to an end and we hear the record hissing and clicking monotonously on the turntable. The blind MATCH-SELLER appears. He fumbles his way to the gramophone and removes the record. Silence. Lights dim to blackout.*

*The watching PILGRIMS applaud as the lights come up.*

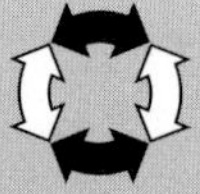

**FREEZE-FRAMING** In groups of four, prepare a sequence of freeze-frames to show the main things that happen at the end of the Pardoner's Tale, from the point where Ronald arrives back.

**STORYBOARDING** Imagine you were making a film of the Pardoner's Tale. Storyboard the last few moments – again from the point where Ronald arrives back at the disused music shop where Johnnie and Cyril are waiting. Sketch out a sequence of frames to show the main shots. Under each frame write down any of the dialogue that is being spoken, and by the side add notes on sound effects or music.

**ARTWORK** The action of the Pardoner's Tale takes place in several different locations, including the gang's headquarters, the market and the music shop. Draw some sketches to show how a simple set could be adapted to represent all of these various locations. Add notes to explain which basic props might be needed (such as chairs or boxes).

**WRITING** Imagine you were a newspaper reporter, who had heard about the discovery of the three bodies. Write the next day's news report. Include details about the other mysterious killings (see page 10) and report some of the rumours and explanations which are going around as to who the killer might be.

**DISCUSSION** In pairs, discuss what evidence there is to back up each of the following statements:
- the 'killer' is not a rival crook;
- the match-seller is some kind of supernatural figure – perhaps Death or Fate;
- the three men are killed by their own greed;
- the moral of the tale is that greed will kill you.

| | |
|---|---|
| **WIFE OF BATH** | Ooh, that made me feel all creepy. |
| **PARDONER** | Probably a bad conscience. (*The WIFE gives the PARDONER a hard look.*) Now, my friends and fellow-sinners… |
| | *He switches to being a fundamentalist preacher, and some of the more credulous PILGRIMS gather round him* |
| | …my message to you today is a simple one: Radix malorum est cupiditas. Or, in our vulgar parlance… |
| **SCHOLAR** | …'The love of money is the root of all evil.' The first Epistle of Paul to Timothy, chapter 6, verse 10. |
| **PARDONER** | The Lord be praised for erudition! Yes, indeed, sinners, the |

270

**fundamentalist preacher** *the Pardoner adopts a very dramatic delivery, frightening the villagers with stories about hell and torment.*

**credulous** *willing to believe anything; easily fooled.*

**erudition** *learning.*

root of all evils. Dig it out of your hearts, friends, eradicate it so that no trace remains behind to befoul and pollute your everlasting souls and ye descend to the pits of Acheron, there to be consumed in sulphurous flames for all eternity. For I say unto you, it is easier for a camel to go through the eye of a needle, than for a rich man to enter the kingdom of God. But, I hear you ask, how can I cast out the devil avarice? To whom should I turn? Where can I find forgiveness?

*Strategic pause to check that they are rapt. Having confirmed that they are, he switches to double-glazing salesman mode.*

Well, this is your lucky day, ladies and gents, because I have here in my capacious bag an incomparable selection of pardons, hot from the Vatican, all signed and sealed by his Holiness Pope Urban VI: venial sins, half a groat; sins of commission, omission and cardinal sins, special terms negotiable. This is the real thing – beware of cheap imitations and buy now while stocks last.

*Hubbub of babbling as the PILGRIMS around him scrabble to snap up his pardons. But he is a keen salesman and notices that some are standing aloof: the WIFE OF BATH has adopted a particularly sceptical pose. He singles her out, shouting over the crowd's noise.*

But one warning I must issue! *(They fall silent.)* If any one of you here has recently been guilty of a sin that you are too

**Acheron** *in classical mythology, one of the rivers of the underworld.*

**Vatican** *in Rome, the capital city of the Roman Catholic church, where the Pope ('his Holiness') lives.*

**venial sins**; **sins of commission**, **omission** *and* **cardinal sins** *different 'grades' of sins.*

**half a groat** *two pence.*

ashamed to admit, then on no account should you approach to buy my pardons. If you are unshriven, having in the past few days committed, let us say, adultery…  **30**

*The crowd around him slowly turns to follow his gaze and there is now a solid block of suspicion directed at the WIFE. She reacts.*

**WIFE OF BATH**  You con-man! You shark! You…

*The HOST steps in.*

**HOST**  Time for the off, ladies and gents! It's April, when sweet showers pierce March's drought, the birdies sing, soft zephyrs blow, we're halfway through Aries, and people like you lot long to go on pilgrimages – *(Sotto voce:)* Goodness only knows why! – *(Full volume:)* So pick up your bags,  **31** tighten your belts and we'll hit Watling Street before the morning rush-hour. To Canterbury, my piously purposeful peregrinators! To Canterbury!

*They respond noisily, pick up their bags and go. As they exit, music accompanies the set-change.*

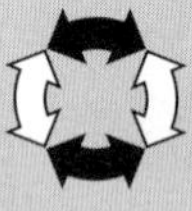

**PERFORMING AND DISCUSSING**  In small groups act out the scene in which the Pardoner extracts money out of the villagers (from 'Ooh, that made me feel all creepy' to 'You shark! You…'). Then talk about the tricks the Pardoner uses to get money out of gullible people.

**if you are unshriven**  *if you have not confessed your sins to a priest and been forgiven.*

**adultery**  *being unfaithful to your marriage partner by having sex with someone else.*

**peregrinators**  *travellers.*

# SCENE 3

*The Red Lion, Dartford. Early morning on day 2 of the pilgrimage.*

*Among other changes to the set, the 'Tabard' sign is removed and a different sign hung elsewhere to let us know that we are in the courtyard of the Red Lion, Dartford. When the music ends, the silence is broken by the sound of the MILLER's lewd guffawing as he descends from an upper room. He is followed by the COOK and seems to be trying to recall a dirty joke. Their noise brings other PILGRIMS out from different corners of the inn.*

| | | |
|---|---|---|
| **MILLER** | Anyway, the old geezer takes his wife to live in a little village just outside Oxford. Nice little cottage… | 1 |
| **COOK** | Two up, two down. | |
| **MILLER** | Two up, as you say, two down; and he settles down to ply his trade… | |
| **COOK** | I know what you mean. | |
| **MILLER** | Right. | |
| **COOK** | What trade was he, by the way? | |
| **MILLER** | I'm coming to that. (*He pretends to take the COOK discreetly out of the REEVE's hearing.*) He's a carpenter. | 10 |
| **REEVE** | I heard that! This is slander! And libel! | |
| **MILLER** | I am simply recounting to my associate here a trifling anecdote concerning a young girl and her wrinkly husband. | |

**slander… libel** *saying untrue and damaging things about someone.*

**trifling anecdote** *insignificant little story.*

---

| | |
|---|---|
| **REEVE** | A carpenter! You said he was a carpenter! *(To the Cook.)* Didn't he? |
| **COOK** | Well… |
| **REEVE** | See! He's getting at me. Ever since we left Southwark, whenever he leaves off playing those obscene bagpipes, he's telling filthy stories. And they're all about carpenters! |
| **MILLER** | No they're not. |
| **COOK** | No. They're not. |
| **MILLER** | It's the same one. I haven't finished it yet. |
| **COOK** | He hasn't started it yet. |
| **LAWYER** | May I make a suggestion? The legal position regarding slander is a minefield. Now, if you want my advice… |
| **REEVE** | Yes? |
| **LAWYER** | It will be fairly expensive. |
| **HOST** | *(Pushing through the crowd.)* Alternatively you can have mine for nothing. Tit for tat's my motto. If you don't like him telling scurrilous stories about carpenters, you tell one about a miller. |
| | *Approval from the PILGRIMS.* |
| **REEVE** | Right! *(He racks his brains.)* |
| **HOST** | Well, go on then. |
| **REEVE** | *(Inspiration!)* Right! |
| | *The PILGRIMS cheer and prepare for…* |

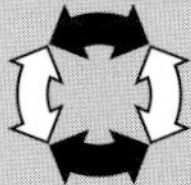

**ARTWORK** Draw a cartoon or sketch to show what the Miller looked like. Here are some more details provided by Chaucer:
- He was muscular, good at wrestling; square-built, broad and thick-set; and was able to heave a door off its hinges;
- He had a red beard, broad like a spade; a wart on the tip of his nose with hairs growing out of it; wide, black nostrils; and a big mouth;
- He carried a sword and small shield; he wore a white coat and a blue hood; and he played the bagpipes.

# *The Reeve's Tale*

**REEVE**  So there's this miller, see…  1

*Cheers of approval, except from the MILLER himself, who sneaks off to console himself with an unsupervised keg.*

Right, and he lives deep in the country, right out in the sticks – not far from Cambridge – with his lovely wife and beautiful daughter. *(More ribald cheers.)* Now he's a typical miller, this character: loud, ill-tempered, uncouth, mouth like a midden, and a crook. They're all the same, millers, and they all try the same scams. You know the kind of thing – your hundredweight of corn goes in one door, and you end  10
up with a sackful of bran at the other.

Anyway, every year this miller grinds the corn for one of them Cambridge colleges. And every year he fleeces 'em. Now, one harvest-time, the old college manciple's ill, see.

**midden** *dung-heap.*

So, in his place they send two young students, John and Alan by name, and they vow that, one way or another, the miller isn't going to get the better of them!

*During this last section of the Reeve's introduction, a film-projector is set up, for the narrative will be acted out in the flickering frames of a silent movie. As he completes his speech, a caption appears, e.g. on a flip-chart placed on one of the upper balconies, reading THE REEVE'S TALE.  Just before the caption appears there is music: the tinkling piano of silent-movie days accompanies the action.*

*Some of the PILGRIMS have formed a couple of lines of cinema*

*audience, and a LATECOMER sidles between them, muttering his
'excuse-me's. The movie is beginning.*

*'On screen', a MILLER enters, sweeping the floor. Behind him,
serving as a back-cloth, three adjoining areas of the structure have
been curtained off.*

*Enter JOHN and ALAN, carrying a sackful of corn. In keeping with
the silent-movie era, they are dressed in twenties boaters and college
scarves. They are welcomed by the MILLER, who is joined by his
WIFE and their simpering DAUGHTER, who relieve the boys of the
corn and exeunt. The MILLER gestures welcomingly to the
STUDENTS…*

*Caption: 'WHY NOT TAKE A NAP WHILE I DO THE WORK?'*

*The BOYS turn down the offer emphatically, much to the MILLER's
obvious annoyance; he storms out.*

*Caption: HALF AN HOUR LATER.*

*The MILLER brings in a sack marked 'grain', dumps it in front of
the BOYS and gestures that he's popping outside.*

*Caption. 'WON'T BE A TICK. NATURE CALLS.'*

*While he is gone, the BOYS check the sack and give a thumbs up to
signify that it's full of grain. Suddenly the MILLER re-enters,
feigning great agitation.*

*Caption: 'ARE YOU AWARE THAT YOUR CAR IS RUNNING
DOWN THE HILL?'*

*The BOYS rush out, the MILLER laughs heartily and the WOMEN
run in with a sack marked 'bran'. They effect the exchange and
disappear, leaving the MILLER to gloat…*

*Caption: 'GOT THE BETTER OF THEM!'*

*The BOYS return, exhausted, dishevelled and despondently carrying
bits of car. The MILLER makes tut-tutting gestures and mock-
sympathetically offers them accommodation:*

*Caption: 'LOOKS AS THOUGH YOU'LL HAVE TO STAY THE NIGHT.'*

*They reluctantly agree and, as the WOMEN enter with a keg of beer, the caption once more indicates the passage of time:*

*Caption: LATER THAT EVENING.*

*They are all drunk. The BOYS help the MILLER to his bed (behind the middle curtain) and then wave goodnight longingly to the DAUGHTER, who retires behind the left-hand curtain. The WIFE watches suspiciously as the boys go behind the right-hand curtain, and then joins the MILLER (whose feet are protruding), having first placed her baby in its cradle at the foot of their bed.*

*The BOYS' curtain opens and JOHN gestures to ALAN that he intends to join the DAUGHTER. He creeps across and disappears behind her curtain. After a second or two, the curtain starts to move and a firework explodes colourfully.*

*Caption: 'OH, MY GOODNESS!'*

*ALAN looks deeply envious. But fate is kind to him. The miller's WIFE emerges, chamber-pot in hand, and exits to empty it. This gives ALAN an idea. He gets out and moves the cradle from the centre bed to his own… The WIFE returns, gropes around at the foot of her bed to check on the baby and, unable to locate the cradle, moves on to Alan's bed, where she stumbles over it.*

*Caption: 'CRUMBS! NEARLY GOT INTO THE WRONG BED!'*

*She enters Alan's bed, where there are similar special effects. At one point ALAN tries to escape, but is dragged back in.*

*Caption: 'WHOOPEE!'*

*A cock crows. JOHN drags himself sleepily from the daughter's bed, intending to return to his own. Stumbling over the cradle, he congratulates himself on a narrow escape:*

*Caption: 'PHEW! THAT WAS A CLOSE SHAVE!'*

*He makes his way back to the middle bed and sits on the edge with the curtain open. Shaking the feet which protrude next to him, he proceeds to regale the occupant of the bed with a graphic description of his night's exploits.*

*Caption: 'WHAT A NIGHT! JUST LISTEN TO THIS…!'*

*Slowly and ominously, the MILLER sits up. JOHN realises his mistake and tries to escape, but the MILLER goes berserk and pins JOHN to the floor. ALAN and the WIFE emerge. She picks up the chamber-pot and mistakenly smashes it over the MILLER's head. As JOHN and ALAN make their escape, the DAUGHTER hands them the stolen grain.*

*Caption: THE END.*

REEVE       So our two young bucks escaped into the dawn.
They'd got their grain – and ground the miller's corn!

*General cheers. CHAUCER and the FRANKLIN are sitting having a drink on one of the balconies. CHAUCER is making notes in a small book.*

FRANKLIN       So you're really going to write these down? I mean, all of them?

CHAUCER       Yes. Why not?

FRANKLIN       Well, one or two are likely to be a bit vulgar, don't you think?

CHAUCER       Looked at in a certain way, yes. But we could hardly expect Oswald to recite selections from The Legend of Good Women, now could we?

FRANKLIN       No. Dreary stuff. *(Thinks.)* Who did write that?

CHAUCER       I did, actually.

**regale** *entertain.*

31

---

| | |
|---|---|
| **FRANKLIN** | I say, I'm terribly sorry. |
| **CHAUCER** | No, that's my whole point. Oswald's tale was excellent of its kind. And who am I to act the censor? I'll simply write them down as they're told and see what we end up with. |
| **FRANKLIN** | Well, we're all looking forward to yours. |
| **CHAUCER** | Mine? |
| **FRANKLIN** | Your tale. We're looking forward to it with eager anticipation. |
| **CHAUCER** | *(Uncertainly.)* Ah, my tale… Yes, I thought you might be… |

*The WIFE OF BATH enters with the SCHOLAR. He looks aghast at a piece of information she has just imparted.*

| | |
|---|---|
| **SCHOLAR** | Five? |
| **WIFE OF BATH** | Yes, five. Does that give you a problem? |
| **SCHOLAR** | No, no, of course not. It's just that… *(scrabbling for an excuse.)* You don't look old enough, for one thing. |
| **WIFE OF BATH** | Sweet boy! |
| **SCHOLAR** | And… Well, you must admit that five husbands is a little excessive. |
| **WIFE OF BATH** | Oh, it's excessive all right. You can't whack a bit of excess. *(Meaningfully.)* Roll on number six, I say! |

*As the SCHOLAR makes his terrified escape, there is music, to cover the change of set which indicates that we have arrived in Rochester.*

---

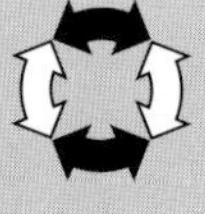

**PERFORMING** In small groups, plan and rehearse a performance of the Reeve's Tale. First work out which simple props you will need and think about the positions of the three beds. Print the captions and find some appropriate music to accompany the action.

# *SCENE 4*

*The Cross Keys, Rochester. Day 3 of the pilgrimage.*

*The NUN enters, accompanied by two pilgrims, MARY and JEAN, who have just 'done' Canterbury and are on their way home. Their clothes and trappings mark them out as returning holiday-makers: the scallop-shell is much in evidence and they almost, but don't quite, wear 'kiss-me-quick' hats. As they chat, they sit the NUN down and encourage her to share in their picnic. Whatever is the medieval equivalent of a thermos-flask – they have it. Being often in each other's company, they have developed a verbal tic which involves repeating odd bits of each other's utterances ('it's lovely…' 'lovely…').*

| | | |
|---|---|---|
| **JEAN** | Oh, I think you ought to be there by Friday. Don't you think so, Mary? Friday at the latest. | 1 |
| **MARY** | Oh, yes. Unless they take the diversion. | |
| **JEAN** | Yes. Sometimes the road's a bit mucky, so they go the other way. | |
| **MARY** | We were fine last week, though. And Kent hasn't had a lot of rain, really. | |
| **JEAN** | March was very dry. | |
| **MARY** | Yes. You shouldn't have much trouble. | |
| **NUN** | I do hope not. I am so looking forward to getting there. | 10 |

**scallop-shell** *the badge that people wore to show that they had been on a pilgrimage.*

**verbal tic** *habit of speech which they can't control.*

| | |
|---|---|
| **MARY** | Oh, it's lovely. We go every year, don't we, Jean? |
| **JEAN** | Every year. Wouldn't miss it. |
| **MARY** | I tell a lie. We did go abroad once, didn't we. Do you remember? |
| **JEAN** | Remember? Never again! |
| **MARY** | When was that? '80? '81? |
| **JEAN** | '81: there was that unpleasantness with the peasants on Blackheath. |
| **MARY** | What a journey! Saint James of Compostella. Spain, you know: *(Over-enunciating.)* Ga-li-thi-a. |
| **JEAN** | Ooh, the food! |
| **MARY** | Never mind the food, dear. What about the men? I don't know what they take us English girls for, I really don't. |
| **JEAN** | Anyway, dear. You stick to Canterbury and you won't have any problems of that nature. |
| **MARY** | No. The weather might not be too reliable, but at least you can get a decent piece of cheese. |
| **NUN** | You were saying – about Canterbury? |
| **JEAN** | Oh, it's lovely! |
| **MARY** | Mind you, you've not picked the nicest time of year. |
| **JEAN** | No, that's true. You can't see it at its best with pilgrims crawling all over. |
| **NUN** | But, surely, the cathedral… |

**'81... Blackheath** *she is referring to the Peasants' Revolt, 1381.*

**Saint James of Compostella** *in Spain; one of the most popular pilgrimage sites in mainland Europe.*

| | |
|---|---|
| **JEAN** | Oh, it's lovely, the cathedral! |
| **NUN** | And quieter than the city streets? |
| **JEAN** | Well again, it depends what time you go, dear. We saw it about… |
| **MARY** | Just after lunch – Tuesday? |
| **JEAN** | No, not Tuesday: we were with those nice people from Halifax. |
| **MARY** | Oh, yes. *(To the now anxious NUN.)* Charming couple. |
| **JEAN** | Wednesday. Wednesday it was, because we had to rush off before the silversmith's closed. |
| **MARY** | So we did. Yes, you ought to be all right if you nip in after lunch midweek. The queue's not too long then. |
| **NUN** | The queue? |
| **MARY** | To see Saint Thomas. The shrine, you know. |
| **NUN** | Yes, I do know what you mean. I just hadn't thought… |
| **MARY** | Oh, yes. There's always a queue. Well, it's how they make their money. And what money! |
| **JEAN** | Last year, in offerings to Saint… Thingy… over nine hundred and fifty pounds. Imagine! |
| | *The NUN gets up.* |
| **MARY** | Are you off, dear? |
| **NUN** | Yes. I think we're about to leave and my Lady Prioress will be needing me. May God give you a safe return to Southwark. |

40

50

**offerings** *pilgrims would donate money in the hope that Saint Thomas would answer their prayers.*

| | |
|---|---|
| **JEAN** | Thank you, dear. I'm sure He will. |
| **MARY** | And you enjoy yourself. Remember – you only get out of a holiday what you put in! |
| **NUN** | I'm sure you're right. *(Exits.)* |
| **MARY** | Nice girl. |
| **JEAN** | Mm. Bit quiet, but nice. Oh, no! |

*She has spotted the SUMMONER. He is inspecting the wares of a street trader and is eating a leek.*

| | |
|---|---|
| **MARY** | What? |
| **JEAN** | Over there. Look! It's him! |
| **MARY** | Who? |
| **JEAN** | That summoner. |
| **MARY** | What? From Sidcup? |
| **JEAN** | Yes. Let's get out of here, quick! |

*She starts agitatedly packing up their picnic things, hastily throwing mugs and food into the basket.*

| | |
|---|---|
| **MARY** | What's he doing here, then? |
| **JEAN** | I don't know, do I? He's with the other lot, I suppose, going the other way. |
| **MARY** | Well, why are you hiding, anyway? |
| **JEAN** | Because I haven't paid my church tithes for six months, that's why! Come on! *(Exeunt.)* |

**tithes** *taxes which had to be paid to the church (a tenth of a person's income).*

*Enter the MILLER in a fury, followed by the COOK.*  **80**

**MILLER**   Oswald!

**COOK**   Calm down!

**MILLER**   Calm down? I'll kill the dirty little… Waits till I'm taking a quiet nap, and then, behind my back – behind my back, mark you…

**COOK**   He was only getting revenge for all those stories you tell about carpenters.

**MILLER**   *(Stops.)* Here. Did I tell you the one about…

**COOK**   Probably. And anyway, you were drunk. You'd never have understood it, even if you had stayed awake.   **90**

**MILLER**   What do you mean, drunk?

**COOK**   Drunk. Tipsy. Intoxicated. Brahms and Liszt. Three sheets in the wind. One over the eight. Squiffy. Sozzled. Wasted. Legless. Inebriated. Nicely thank you. Pie-eyed, pickled, plastered and palatic. Tight as a Gosport fiddler. Wazzocked.

**MILLER**   *(Threateningly.)* I was tired.

**COOK**   All right. You were tired.

**MILLER**   Right. *(Exit.)*

**COOK**   Tired as a newt. *(Exit.)*

*Enter the HOST, followed by the rest of the PILGRIMS.*   **100**

**HOST**   Gather round, everybody! It's time for the professional!

**CHAUCER**   *(Extremely nervous and reluctant.)* Ah, now, I'm not altogether…

**HOST**   *(Overriding CHAUCER's reluctance.)* Mr Chaucer's going to dig deep into his wealth of literature and erudition, and it's odds on he'll come up with a stunner. He needs no introduction. Author of such well-known works as *(Surreptitiously consulting* a scrap of paper.) The ABC of the Virgin, *(Approving nods from the Prioress's entourage; puzzlement from everyone else.)* The Parliament of Fowls, *(More widespread recognition.)* and that best-selling bodice-ripper Troilus and Criseyde, *(Gasps.)* I give you – Mr Geoffrey Chaucer!

**CHAUCER**   *(Nervously producing some messy sheets of paper.)* Thank you. Most kind. Er, this is a little metrical romance addressing the topic of knighthood. In it I propose... Well, here it is: Sir Topaze.

**WRITING**  Reread the scene between Mary, Jean and the Nun, and jot down what their conversation tells us about Canterbury Cathedral at that time, and pilgrimages. Make notes on: travelling; the route to Canterbury; the popularity of this particular pilgrimage; what it is like inside the cathedral; the shrine of St Thomas; how much money the cathedral takes from pilgrims. Then write an entry in the Nun's diary for that evening, in which she records her conversation with the two pilgrims and expresses her reactions to it.

**LANGUAGE STUDY**  A synonym is a word which has the same – or almost the same – meaning as another word. Can you add more synonyms for 'drunk' to the list that the Cook provides on page 37? Most of them will probably be slang expressions.

**The ABC...** *These were all titles of Chaucer's books.*

**bodice-ripper** *sensational story about sex, set in the past.*

# *Chaucer's Tale of Sir Topaze*

*The HOST motions the PILGRIMS to create a wide acting space, and CHAUCER takes up a position rather like the one he adopted for the painting of him reading to the court of Richard II – very stiff and formal. As he recites, the story is acted out.*

*It is introduced by some recorded music: the signature tune 'Music while you work'.*

**CHAUCER**　　　Now, listen everyone, I pray,　　　　　　　　　1
And I will tell you, if I may,
Of a hero, strong and bold.
Try to imagine, if you can,
A truly perfect gentleman;
Sir Topaze, he was called.

*The setting is mid-twentieth century. SIR TOPAZE enters on a bike. He is dressed in pin-stripe suit and bowler hat, with umbrella, The Times, etc. Topaze's FATHER pushes on an armchair. MUM kisses him and takes his bicycle clips.*　　　10

Sir Topaze was a splendid chap,
White was his face as milkmaid's cap,
His lips were pink as rose.
His beard was full and bushy red
And in the middle of his head
There grew a handsome nose.

*TOPAZE sits in the armchair. MUM coddles him – takes his jacket and shoes off, etc., provides slippers and puts his feet on a pouffe.*

The maidens living far and near
All thought Sir Topaze was a dear　　　　　　　　　20
And wished that he would come
To visit them and have a chat;
But he preferred to stroke his cat
And stay home with his mum.

*MUM brings in a sackful of post and hands him the top envelope –
an enormous Valentine. TOPAZE reads it, laughs scornfully and
throws it over his shoulder.*

But every weekend he would go
Abroad to seek a valiant foe
And fight in mortal combat.
He'd stiffen like a tiger grim,
A lion was no match for him –
He'd even scare a wombat!

*DAD brings in a television. TOPAZE mimes enthusiastically
watching a football match. Puzzled and somewhat cheated cries from
the PILGRIMS: 'Wombat? What the hell's a wombat?' etc.*

**CHAUCER**     Well, I'm not sure actually… But I had difficulty finding a
rhyme for 'combat', you see…

*He gives an embarrassed cough and forges on…*

And then one day he shook with fear:
A challenge came with message clear
To see who was the best –
Sir Topaze with his laurel crown
Or White-clad Giant from Kingston Town:
Now this would be the Test!

*The POSTMAN enters and hands TOPAZE a worryingly official-
looking letter. MUM and DAD and the POSTMAN stand waiting in
trepidation as TOPAZE opens it… He staggers back on reading the
contents…*

But Topaze was a fighter bold
And would not flinch, as you've been told,
From going out to battle;
He knew the deed had to be done,
He would not fly, nor 'scape, nor run;
This giant would not rattle
*(Lamely.)* him.
And so he called for armour strong

And weapons sharp and hard and long
To fight the giant grim.

*Left alone, TOPAZE thrusts back his shoulders resolutely and takes a*     **60**
*few deep breaths. He calls: 'Mum!'*

They brought him first some cool red wine
The sweetest crushings of the vine
To keep his spirits high;
With pheasant, game and other meat,
As much boar's head as he could eat,
The best that gold could buy.

*MUM brings in a mug of tea and adds several sugar-lumps – then*
*whisky. DAD brings in fish and chips in newspaper. TOPAZE swiftly*
*consumes a portion of each.*     **70**

He then did doff his tunic black
Which erstwhile graced his comely back
As straight as any rod;
And then removed his nether dress,
When – lo! In all his nakedness
He stood there like a god!

*Removes waistcoat. Slips off braces. Removes trousers, to reveal long*
*coms. Scratches his tummy.*

They brought him then his battle-wear:
Some snow-white leggings, passing fair     **80**
To clothe his comely thighs.
There never was another knight
Whose pins were such a splendid sight –
I tell you folk no lies!

**doff**  *take off.*

**erstwhile**  *previously.*

**coms**  *'combinations' (vest and long pants all in one).*

*MUM and DAD bring his cricket whites. He slips on the trousers (braces in England team colours already attached).*

And then each of his legs receives
One half a pair of snow-white greaves;
And now perhaps he'll manage
To face whate'er the giant grim
Might in his wrath propel at him,
Without excessive damage.

*Buckles on his pads.*

His coat of arms is donned and tied,
For Topaze wears it with great pride,
It truly may be said.
And then, to save him from the shock
Of flying stone or bouncing rock,
A helmet for his head.

*Slips on England tie (already knotted and matching the braces). Dons cap to match.*

With gauntlets girt, Topaze is set;
There just remains one thing to get
And then he'll never yield.
For, last of all, to save his parts
From jealous spears or envy's darts –
Topaze's trusty shield!

*MUM ceremoniously brings in his cricket box on a cushion. DAD takes it equally ceremoniously and thrusts it into TOPAZE's trousers. There is a suspicion of a wince.*

He takes his battered sword in hand,
He'll leave his own beloved land,

**greaves** *armour to protect the shins.*

**gauntlets girt** *wearing gloves.*

**cricket box** *a hard protector to cover the groin.*

All thoughts of home are gone.
For he must journey now to meet
A foe that he would fain not greet
In distant Kennington.

*Collects his bat. Takes leave of his weeping MUM and stiff-upper-lip DAD.*

The pilgrimage is long and tough,
But Topaze has not had enough –
He knows the giant is waiting.
And in good time our knight serene
Takes up his stand upon the green,
His courage not abating.

**120**

*He walks out to the crease. Takes guard with the assistance of the UMPIRE (the POSTMAN doubling).*

**abating** *fading away.*

The air is filled with fearful sounds
Of clashing armour all around –
All this Sir Topaze hears.
And then a thundering of hooves
Like cannon-balls on castle roofs,
As White-clad Giant appears!

*Sound effects of the West Indian supporters rhythmically clanking tin cans. Steel bands playing in the background.*

*A huge West Indies BOWLER enters, rubbing the ball menacingly on his trousers. His feet paw the ground threateningly, as he sizes up his opponent. He walks back to start his run-up…*

*Suddenly there is a terrific flash and a crash of thunder, followed by the sound of torrential rain. TOPAZE, the BOWLER and the UMPIRE all look despondently heavenwards, shrug their shoulders and walk off together as the signature tune ('Music while you work') fades in. They return, with MUM and DAD, to take their curtain-call.*

*CHAUCER bows as the PILGRIMS applaud somewhat half-heartedly.*

**HOST**          Is that it?

**CHAUCER**       Well… yes.

**HOST**          That's diabolical! I mean, it didn't get anywhere.

**FRANKLIN**      Oh, it wasn't that bad.

**HOST**          Yes it was!

*A debate ensues which threatens to get a bit lively until it is interrupted by the HOST's loud reminder that it is time for them to resume the pilgrimage.*

**HOST**          Off we go, then! Nice leisurely little leg today. *(Fairly politely, to the Prioress.)* Come on, madam, the horses are waiting! Ten miles to Sittingbourne – we can get in a couple of tales on the way. *(Less politely to one of the others.)* Move! Let's be having you…

*As they leave, music to represent the next leg of the pilgrimage. As it plays, the PILGRIMS mime the journey, re-entering to pass across the stage in groups or singly, each person walking or riding in a characteristic fashion. Features of the set change to indicate the departure from Rochester and the passage through various villages on the way to Sittingbourne. When all have crossed once, they re-enter and halt on the HOST's imperious cry.*

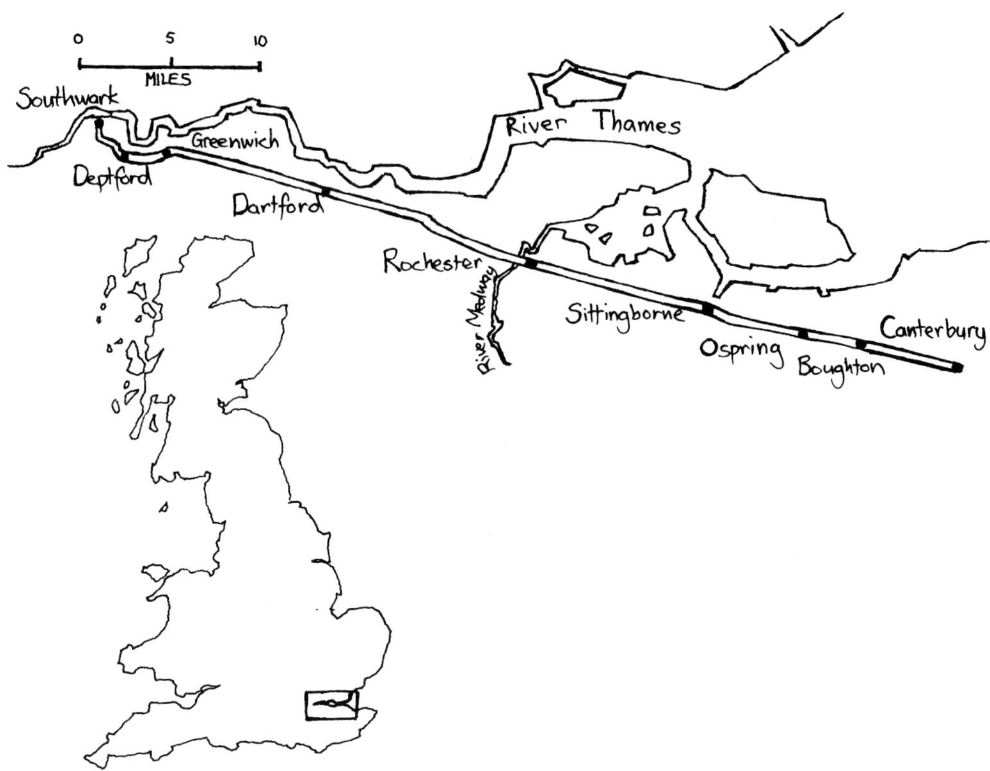

 **PERFORMING**  In small groups, make a list of the props and costumes needed for Chaucer's tale of Sir Topaze. Collect together as many as you can and perform the tale, with one person reading the verse as Chaucer while others act out each scene. You might want to have music playing in the background (and don't forget the sound effects – which you can make yourselves, 'live').

**WRITING**  In the play about Sir Topaze, we hear Chaucer telling us a story about a knight of old going out to fight a giant, while we are actually watching a cricketer preparing to play in a test match. Write the opening (or more, if you can) of a similar play. For example, you could have someone reading out a fairy tale or an ancient myth, while we watch a very different and modern version of the story being acted out.

**READING**  By now you ought to be able to list a number of Chaucer's 'works', or writings. Make a list which starts with *The Canterbury Tales* and add other titles from Chaucer's conversation with the Franklin on page 31 and the Host's introduction to Chaucer's tale on page 38.

**ARTWORK**  Draw a larger version of the map on page 45, which shows the route that the pilgrimage would have taken. Add to your map (i) the days of the journey so far (for example, write 'Day 1' next to Southwark); (ii) the names of the inns they stay in; and (iii) the titles of the tales which have been told on different days. (The order of the tales in this play version is different from Chaucer's.) Save your map so that you can add to it later.

# SCENE 5

*The Dolphin, Sittingbourne. Day 4 of the pilgrimage.*

**HOST**  Lunch break!  1

*CHAUCER and the FRANKLIN seem to have become friends. As people sit around eating and drinking, they share a loaf of bread and some wine.*

**CHAUCER**  Got any children?

**FRANKLIN**  Yes, one… *(Pause; subdued.)* Bit of a disappointment to be honest. Bad company – you know the kind of thing. Never see him with anybody you might call – for want of a better word – a gentleman.

**HOST**  *(Who has been listening in.)* Gentleman? What the hell's that  10
got to do with anything? This is 1385, Franklin. We can't go on living in the past for ever, you know. I mean jousting's all very nice, and writing poetry and playing the flute; but it's not going to pay the rent in the real world, is it?

**FRANKLIN**  No, I suppose not. But that wasn't what I really meant by 'gentleman'. *(To CHAUCER.)* I think a good parent or good son is a bit like a good husband or wife. It's largely a question of compromises and understanding.

**HOST**  I still fail to see what that's got to do with being a 'gentleman'.  20

*The FRANKLIN pauses, breathes deeply, and begins his tale.*

**jousting**  *combat between two knights on horseback, often engaged in as a kind of sport.*

**compromises**  *give and take.*

# *The Franklin's Tale*

| | |
|---|---|
| **FRANKLIN** | There was once, in a distant place, at a distant time, a husband and wife. Their story begins with a leave-taking… |

*Music, played on the sitar.*

*The scene is India at the height of the Raj. Sounds of a barrack-square outside. GUS, an officer, is buckling on the last of his uniform, assisted by his young wife, DOROTHEA. For a moment they stand looking at each other. A SOLDIER enters.*

| | |
|---|---|
| **SOLDIER** | Captain Osborne says we're ready for the off, sir. |
| **GUS** | Thank you, Corporal. |

*There is a brief silence after the CORPORAL leaves.*

I'll drop you a line as soon as we reach Chini.

| | |
|---|---|
| **DORRIE** | Yes. |
| **GUS** | You'll be amazed how quickly the time will pass. |
| **DORRIE** | Oh, I'm sure it will. Tiffin with Mildred and endless evenings of bridge with the Brigadier's wife. |
| **GUS** | Yes. Looked at in that way, where I'm going does seem less grim! |

*They manage a laugh.*

I must go.

---

**the Raj** *the period in the nineteenth century when India was part of the British Empire.*

**tiffin** *the army name for lunch or tea in India at that time.*

*They kiss and he leaves quickly. We hear the band strike up and a
series of barked orders. She runs up to the balcony and waves.*

*As the brass-band music fades, to be replaced by a subdued string
quartet, the watching PILGRIMS part to reveal a whist party in
progress.*

**BRIGADIER'S WIFE**  Where's Dorothea? You did invite her, didn't you, Mildred?

**MILDRED**  She might not come. I think she's still missing her husband
rather. She worries a great deal, you know, and I have the
feeling she finds company rather trying.

**BRIGADIER'S WIFE**  Well, we can only do our best. And she has to learn that
being an army wife means separations – it's one of the
sacrifices we have to make.

**MRS JOPLIN**  Frankly, I've always enjoyed it. Now that Bernard's been
promoted, he's a confounded nuisance. Under my feet all the
time: interfering with servants…

**BRIGADIER'S WIFE**  Yes, I know what you mean. I think it does a husband and
wife good to be apart for a while – makes the heart grow
fonder, and all that sort of thing. And certainly in Dorothea's
case she has very little to be anxious about. According to
Charles, Gus did an excellent job with that rebellion on the
islands. His present duties can't be much more than the odd
bit of administration. He certainly isn't in any danger from
the natives any more.

**MILDRED**  No, I think she recognises that. She's more concerned about
the voyage home.

**BRIGADIER'S WIFE**  Ah, yes.

**MILDRED**  The loss of the 'Charlotte' last month made her infinitely
more tense than the casualties in the rebellion ever did. I
suppose she knew that at least Gus had some control over
that. There's not a lot you can do when your ship's being
hurled against the Kotegarh rocks.

**MRS JOPLIN**  And they've barely started work on the lighthouse. In low water those rocks are a death-trap. Mildred, you must remember…

*She has failed to notice DOROTHEA's entrance and the BRIGADIER'S WIFE has to cover the awkwardness.*

**BRIGADIER'S WIFE**  (*Getting up quickly.*) Dorothea! We were just talking about you, weren't we, Mildred? Let's go and find a drink, and you can tell me all the exciting news about Gus's return. It must be soon… (*Relieved.*) Ah, here's Peter. Peter, I have a young lady in distress who is absolutely dying for a drink. I'm sure you won't mind escorting her.

**DORRIE**  Oh, no, really… I…

*But the BRIGADIER'S WIFE has returned to the bridge table. For a moment they stand awkwardly.*

**PETER**  Well, would you like a drink? Or are we going to stand here like statues for the rest of the evening?

**DORRIE**  I asked you not to talk to me again.

**PETER**  I can hardly avoid it when I'm forced upon you by my aunt. Very forceful woman, Aunt Agnes.

**DORRIE**  Look, just leave me alone, will you? I don't want a scene in public.

**PETER**  So what do you want?

**DORRIE**  I'll tell you what I want. I want you to stop pestering me. I want my husband to finish in the islands. I want him home again safe and sound. I want someone to get rid of the infernal Kotegarh rocks! But, we can't all have what we want, can we, Peter?

**PETER**  I'd do anything for you, Dorrie.

**DORRIE**  Don't call me Dorrie.

**PETER**  Anything.

*Pause.*

| DORRIE | All right. Do one thing for me and I'm yours. You have my solemn oath. |
|---|---|
| PETER | Name it. |
| DORRIE | Get rid of the Kotegarh rocks. |
| PETER | I see. There being no dragons left alive to slay, my task is the Kotegarh rocks. |
| DORRIE | You could look at it in that way, yes. The difference is that knights of old had a chance to kill their dragon: yours is an impossibility! |

90

*She turns and goes. The string quartet fades to be replaced by the sound of the sitar, which continues over the dialogue. PETER has not moved, but now an Indian FAKIR stands before him.*

FAKIR
The Kotegarh rocks?

PETER
Yes.

FAKIR
Very difficult.

PETER
Impossible.

FAKIR
No. very difficult. And very expensive. Come.

*In the sequence which follows the FAKIR completes a sequence of magic rituals, which culminate in a flash of coloured smoke. The sitar music suddenly ends and there is a brief silence. Then, almost imperceptibly at first but growing louder, the sound of rain.*

PETER
What's that?

FAKIR
You cannot have lived in India long if you do not know the sound of the monsoon. This year it will be heavy. The waters will rise. The Kotegarh rocks will be no more. Take your lady to the shore. She will see no rocks. And she will not understand. Take her. And when you have had her, bring me my ten thousand rupeees.

PETER
You'll get your money.

*Brief snatch of sitar music. The lights fade to leave PETER in a single spot. When they come up again, the FAKIR has gone and DORRIE stands next to PETER.*

Yes. The rocks are gone.

---

**fakir**  *a holy man.*

**monsoon**  *the heavy seasonal rains which sweep parts of India and other countries.*

| | |
|---|---|
| **DORRIE** | But how on earth…? |
| **PETER** | You don't need to know. That wasn't part of our bargain. Is your husband's ship in yet? |
| **DORRIE** | Yes. He'll be here within the hour. My God, what a homecoming! |
| **PETER** | I'll leave you then. Come to my quarters at ten. |
| **DORRIE** | Oh, Peter! |
| **PETER** | Or I shall spread this whole business around the entire station. You gave your word! |

*He goes. Music and lights down to a spot, as before. When they fade up, GUS is standing next to her.*

| | |
|---|---|
| **GUS** | You gave your word? |
| **DORRIE** | It was a game. A stupid challenge to frighten him off. I never thought it might be possible. |
| **GUS** | So you have to break your word – in which case he will create a scandal, or go to him. |
| **DORRIE** | Or kill myself. |
| **GUS** | Dorrie! |
| **DORRIE** | It's the only honourable way out, Gus. What's the only decent thing to do when a fellow's accused of cowardice or dishonouring the regiment in some way? He goes quietly into his study, he locks the door, takes his revolver out of its holster… |
| **GUS** | No, Dorrie! |
| **DORRIE** | There's nothing left, Gus. I'm dishonoured whatever I do. You said it yourself. Either I break my word, or my marriage vows to you. |
| **GUS** | So it's clear, then. |

120

130

140

*Music. Lights fade to a spot on DORRIE. When they come up, she is with PETER.*

PETER    What are you doing here?

DORRIE    What do you mean – what am I doing here? I've come. I have kept my word. He sent me.

PETER    You told him?

DORRIE    Of course I told him. He's my husband.

PETER    And he let you come?

DORRIE    *(She pauses, thinking it out.)* Gus has never been a great intellectual – I expect you know that. And he could scarcely be regarded as a moral philosopher either. But he does pride himself in doing his job to the best of his ability. And he does follow a no doubt old-fashioned but extremely clear-cut code of conduct, which boils down, I suppose, to being 'decent' to people. *(Putting the following expressions, as it were, in inverted commas:)* Not taking advantage of them when the chips are down. Keeping your word. Playing the game.

PETER    Tell me one thing. When we first met – before all this started – you did have some respect for me, didn't you?

DORRIE    I did, yes. Ironically, I saw many of Gus's qualities in you. At least, I thought I did.

PETER    I want to try to show you that you weren't mistaken. Regain a little self-respect. *(Pause.)* Go back to your husband. Say that I have released you. Tell him that, at least in the end, I have tried to behave like a gentleman.

*Music and lights down to a spot as before. Lights up to show PETER with the FAKIR.*

**moral philosopher** *someone who thinks deeply about right and wrong.*

|  | You're going to have to wait for your ten thousand rupees, I'm afraid. You'll get your money, but I'm going to have to sell a few things first. I simply haven't got that amount of cash. | **170** |

**FAKIR**      Nor the lady, it seems.

**PETER**      How the hell did you know that? If you've been spying on me…

**FAKIR**      I don't need to spy to know that she confided in her husband; that her husband sent her back to you; and that you, in an attempt to match their magnanimity, sent her back again. It was perhaps your attempt to behave as a true officer and gentleman?      **180**

**PETER**      How dare you sneer at me! But I suppose I wouldn't expect your type to understand.

**FAKIR**      I do not sneer. And I understand perfectly – perhaps rather better than you, my friend. I understand that, to be a gentleman in the true sense, one does not have to be a British officer; nor, dare I say it, even British. And, had you been a gentleman, you would not have referred insultingly to 'my type'.

**PETER**      I'm sorry.      **190**

**FAKIR**      I believe you. But now, how does a humble Indian respond in such a situation? Does he insist upon his bond? Or does he too enter the contest to see who can behave in the most gentlemanly fashion? *(Brief dramatic pause.)* Keep your rupees. Forget your debt. Only remember to be – how strange our English language is – a 'gentleman'. Whatever that extraordinary word means.

**magnanimity** *generosity of spirit.*

*Concluding music.*

**FRANKLIN**    You see, the way I view it, the husband, the lover, the magician – they were all 'gentlemanly' in the end – as I understand the term, anyway. So was the wife, though we might find a different word for it. I simply leave you with the question: who was the most generous, in your opinion? The Soldier, the Wife, the Lover or the Magician?

*An animated discussion breaks out among the PILGRIMS, but is interrupted by the arrival of the PARDONER, surrounded by a small crowd of the more credulous PILGRIMS and LOCAL VILLAGERS. One of them carries a small table which will become the PARDONER's stall.*

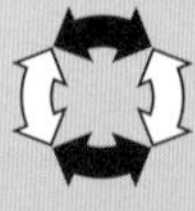

**DISCUSSION**  Hold a class discussion on who you think was the most generous in the Franklin's Tale: the soldier, the wife, the lover or the magician. Before you start the discussion, check back through the story to see how much of a sacrifice each one was prepared to make.

**DISCUSSION**  As a second part of your class discussion, decide what you think the Franklin means by being a 'gentleman'. Make a list of the qualities that you think such a person (male or female) should have in the modern world. (For example, you might start off with generosity…) Chaucer used the word 'gentil' to describe a person who possessed these qualities. Today we might say that such a person was generous, fair and understanding. Can you find or invent a word which brings together all of these qualities, one which can apply equally to men and women, and to people of any origin?

**WRITING**  Write the diary of one of the pilgrims as they stop for the night in the inn. Give their reactions to some of the other pilgrims, to the journey, and to the tales they have heard so far. Write in a style that suits your chosen pilgrim.

# SCENE 6

*During the hubbub there has been music, and a sign now shows
that we are outside The Angel, Boughton. It is early on day 5, the
final day of the journey to Canterbury.*

**PARDONER**    Et eadem auctoritate te absolvo ab omnibus et singulis    1
criminibus delectis et peccatis tuis quantumcumque gravibus
et enormibus. In nomine patris et filii et spiritus sancti.
Amen.

And that'll be half a sovereign, thank you very much. *(Ting!)*
Next!

Indulgences! Hot from the Holy father! Be absolved of your
sins through a share of the heavenly treasury of the mercy of
God, plus a small financial investment. All takings go
straight into the meagre coffers of the mother Church to    10
succour the poor and needy.

And remember, for a clean soul, friends: Purchased
Penitence Washes Whitest!

*As someone buys a pardon, and the PARDONER adds a few more
words of Latin, the DOCTOR and the FRIAR observe his methods.*

**Et eadem...** *And I absolve you (free you) by that same authority
from each and every chosen crime and from your sins, however
grave and serious they might be. In the name of the Father, and the
Son and the Holy Ghost. Amen.*

**succour** *help, support.*

**penitence** *feeling sorry for what you have done; regretting your
sins.*

---

Dominus noster Iesus Cristus per suam piissimam misericordiam te absolvat – ta very much – Et auctoritate eius et beatorum Petri et Pauli apostolorum, ego te absolvo…

**DOCTOR**　　How much of that do you reckon they can understand?

**FRIAR**　　Oh, he might as well be reciting a recipe for spotted dick – they wouldn't know the difference.

**PARDONER**　　But this being a very special sin, my daughter, we need a special absolution.

**GULLIBLE VILLAGER**　　A special…?

**PARDONER**　　For the most insignificant of contributions –

**GULLIBLE VILLAGER**　　I haven't got much…

**PARDONER**　　A mere three groats – you may touch one of my holy relics!

**FRIAR**　　Oh, no! Not the relics!

*As they eagerly crowd round…*

**PARDONER**　　No, please – do not approach too closely. These relics have been preserved through the centuries, finally coming to rest, by God's grace, in the Chapel of the Blessed Mary of

---

**Dominus noster…** *Our Lord Jesus Christ absolves you through his compassionate mercy… And by His authority and that of the blessed apostles Saint Peter and Saint Paul, I absolve you.*

**spotted dick** *a kind of steamed pudding with raisins in.*

**absolution** *the act of officially forgiving someone's sins.*

**three groats** *twelve pence.*

**holy relics** *items such as bones, supposedly connected with saints, martyrs and other holy figures; for example, pardoners would often claim to have bits of the 'true cross' on which Christ was crucified.*

Roncevalles at Charing. They are of inestimable worth and incalculable power. This *(Producing a sheep's bone.)* is the shoulder-bone of Jacob! Dip this in the water of any well, and the sheep and cattle will thrive and multiply. *(Selecting a piece of cloth.)* And what is this?

**FRIAR**    A pillow-case!

**PARDONER**    Yes, sinners, this is no less than Our Lady's veil! And this… a tiny fragment from the sail of Saint Peter's boat. What a state of preservation! They don't make them like they used to! This… the very washing-up bowl used at the Last Supper… And what about one of the Angel Gabriel's wing-feathers? And… *(Dramatically producing two fig-leaves.)* I need hardly tell you who wore these! They are, of course, in the higher price-range, but I have assorted saints' bones to suit the more modest pocket.

*He produces a jar full of bones and tips them on to the table.*

Take your pick, my friends! Empty your purse and save your soul!

*He confidently leaves the stall and approaches the FRIAR, DOCTOR and SUMMONER.*

**FRIAR**    Another good day's takings? *(The PARDONER simply chuckles.)*

**SUMMONER**    You can't complain. You don't see too many poor friars, do

**Roncevalles**  *near Charing Cross in London there was a nunnery connected with the convent of Our Lady of Roncevalles in Spain; pardoners were frequent visitors.*

**Jacob**  *the story of Jacob, including his dealings with sheep and cattle, is told the book of Genesis in the Bible.*

**Last Supper**  *when Jesus ate with his apostles for the final time.*

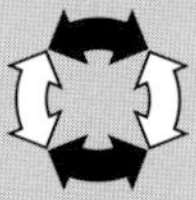

**WRITING** The Pardoner must have used his imagination, collecting and making fake relics. Draw up two columns: in the first, write down what the Pardoner claims that each of his relics is; in the second, explain what each one actually was. Then add some ideas of your own. Think about the kinds of relics that people would have bought, and work out how you could make fake versions. Finally write a short speech by the Pardoner in which he tries to sell these 'newly acquired' relics.

|  |  |
|---|---|
|  | you, Hubert? Your lady friends aren't short of a penny or two. |
| **DOCTOR** | And from what you told me earlier, Summoner… |
| **SUMMONER** | Now, wait a minute… |
| **DOCTOR** | Collecting fines and splitting them fifty-fifty with the archdeacon… |
| **SUMMONER** | That was in confidence to my doctor! |
| **DOCTOR** | I'll keep your secrets. When all's said and done, the whole world's on the fiddle! |
|  | *Their discussion is interrupted by the awful discord of the Miller's bagpipes. The remaining PILGRIMS enter on the final leg of their journey, with the MILLER bringing up the rear. They are exhausted and some remove their shoes to rub sore and blistered feet.* |
| **HOST** | Oh, give it a break, Robin! |
| **MILLER** | Fella's gotta practise. |

**Your lady friends** *Friars had gained a reputation for their activities with women.*

**the archdeacon** *many Summoners would collect fines (for not attending church, for example) and, instead of handing them in, would split them with the archdeacon, the senior priest who ran the local church court.*

| | | |
|---|---|---|
| **LAWYER** | I think I prefer him drunk. | **70** |
| **MILLER** | That's a thought. Gotta mouth as dry as a reeve's wallet… | |
| **REEVE** | He's doing it again! | |
| **LAWYER** | Calm down, Oswald. You had your turn earlier. You got your retaliation in first, remember? | |
| **HOST** | Did he ever finish that joke about the carpenter? | |
| **COOK** | He hasn't stayed sober long enough to remember the ending yet. | |
| **HOST** | So what about it, Robin? I think we're after the watershed. | |
| **MILLER** | What about what? | |
| **HOST** | The Miller's Tale. | **80** |

*Though the PRIORESS and some of the quieter PILGRIMS ostentatiously leave, most of them call out for 'the Miller's Tale', and he swells with pride and enthusiasm.*

| | |
|---|---|
| **MILLER** | The Miller's Tale. Right. Well, as I've been trying to tell you, there's this old carpenter, see. *(Half-hearted complaints from the REEVE are easily quelled.)* and 'e goes an' marries this really gorgeous little young piece, right? And they set up home in a nice little flat above his workshop… |
| **COOK** | Little two-up, two-down… |
| **MILLER** | Right – all alone except for a lodger… *(Obvious reactions from the rowdier PILGRIMS.)* …Yeh, bit of an artist 'e was, and 'e 'ad 'is eye on the carpenter's young wife from the moment 'e set foot in the 'ouse… |

**watershed** *the time in the evening when television programmes can show more 'adult' material.*

**ostentatiously** *they make sure everybody sees that they are leaving in protest.*

# *The Miller's Tale*

*Music: something like 'Jealousy' in French/accordion style.*

*NICOLAS sits sketching ALICE as she tidies the dinner table. When the music develops into something like a tango, he grabs her and they perform a violent and dramatic dance, during which ALICE's head is bashed on the table more than once. The music ends. They reluctantly draw apart. As she straightens her clothes (tight skirt and top; cheeky beret), and NICOLAS goes back to his sketching, enter the older husband, JEAN-PIERRE. When they speak, their accents are exaggeratedly French: a sort of Inspector Clouseau meets 'Allo 'Allo. To maintain the comic-book style, their gestures are melodramatic and extreme, and most of the props they use are two-dimensional flats.*

**JEAN-PIERRE**  (*Suspiciously eyeing the plate.*) 'Allo. 'Ow come ma saucisse is squashed again?

**ALICE**  Jean-Pierre! All you ever think about is your saucisse!

**JEAN-PIERRE**  (*He snatches up his sausage and brandishes it defiantly.*) A man 'as to 'ave an interest!

*Suddenly his eye is caught by something in the newspaper. He flourishes it triumphantly.*

Regarde! 'Sagittarius: You may feel a little flattened today.'

**Inspector Clouseau**  *the French detective played in films by Peter Sellers.*

**'Allo 'Allo**  *a television comedy set in occupied France during the Second World War.*

**melodramatic**  *very overdone.*

**ma saucisse**  *my sausage.*

Hein? 'Oo say ze 'oroscopes lie, hein?

*And he storms out. NICOLAS rushes to ALICE and embraces her*   **10**
*from behind.*

| | |
|---|---|
| **NICOLAS** | Alice! |
| **ALICE** | Nicolas! |
| **NICOLAS** | Alice! |
| **ALICE** | Nicolas! |
| **NICOLAS** | Je t'adore! |
| **ALICE** | Shut it yourself. |
| **NICOLAS** | Mais, non. I love you. |
| **ALICE** | Oh, Nicolas! |
| **NICOLAS** | Oh, Alice!   **20** |
| **ALICE** | *(Dramatically flinging herself from him and taking up a decorative pose elsewhere.)* It is impossible: 'e is always 'ere. |
| **NICOLAS** | *(Thinks.)* Alice? |
| **ALICE** | Nicolas? |
| **NICOLAS** | I 'ave a ruse. |
| **ALICE** | A what? |
| **NICOLAS** | A ruse. A déception. We will trick 'im. |
| **ALICE** | But 'ow? |

**'oroscopes** *horoscopes: predictions based upon 'reading' the stars.*

**Je t'adore** *I love you! (It needs the correct French pronunciation for the joke to work!)*

**ruse** *trick.*

| | |
|---|---|
| **NICOLAS** | Zis – 'ow you say? – astrology. 'E believe, yes? |
| **ALICE** | Mais, d'accord. You 'ave seen 'im. |
| **NICOLAS** | Bien. I ascend to my room. Bring me some food and wine. I may 'ave to remain zere a couple of days. |

*His enigmatic exit and ALICE's puzzlement are exaggeratedly acted out and enhanced by some dramatic bursts of accordian music. During which, lights down and up again to reveal JEAN-PIERRE. He is eating, drinking wine and talking all at the same time.*

| | |
|---|---|
| **JEAN-PIERRE** | Where is Nicolas? |
| **ALICE** | I do not know. I 'ave not seen 'im since two days. |
| **JEAN-PIERRE** | *(Pause as his mental cogs turn and he comes to a decision.)* I go to 'ave a look. |

*They climb to Nicolas's room and pull back the curtain to reveal NICOLAS, sitting in some kind of trance, surrounded by astrological charts, globes, telescopes and calculations on paper.*

Sacré bleu! Zut alors! Dieu et mon droit!

**ALICE**   Ah! Il est mort!

**JEAN-PIERRE**   (*Listening to his chest.*) Non! 'E breathes!

**NICOLAS**   (*'Waking', as ALICE pats his hand solicitously.*) Ah! All is lost!

**JEAN-PIERRE**   What is it that you mean – lost?

**NICOLAS**   Tout est perdu! Ze world is coming to an end! It is written in ze stars!   50

**JEAN-PIERRE**   'Ow? When?

**NICOLAS**   A great flood. Un déluge! Thursday soir. It will cover ze 'ole world! (*As though suddenly seeing a way out.*) Unless…

**JEAN-PIERRE**   Unless? Unless quoi?

**NICOLAS**   Noah! 'E escape ze flood. (*A further 'sudden realisation'.*) You are a carpenter! I tell you what to do. We will be saved!

**MILLER**   So 'e tells this carpenter to string up three wooden tubs from the rafters – one for 'imself, and one each for the lodger and the young wife – (*As the MILLER describes this, we see it happening.*) and then fill 'em up with provisions. Anyway,   60
Thursday night comes, and there's the carpenter, sitting in 'is tub, waiting for Noah's flood to come again; and there's

**Sacré bleu! Zut alors!** *Expressions of surprise often uttered by French characters in comics.*

**Dieu et Mon Droit** *'God and my right': the motto under the royal coat of arms.*

**Il est mort** *he is dead.*

**Tout est perdu** *all is lost.*

**déluge** *flood; Nicolas is trying to persuade the superstitious carpenter that Noah's Flood is coming again; in the Bible, God sent a flood to drown the world, but he instructed Noah to build an ark to save his family and specimens of all animals.*

Alice and Nicolas waiting for 'im to doze off... *(The CARPENTER snores obligingly.)* Which very soon 'e does... And as soon as 'e's fast asleep, they creep out of their tubs...

**DISCUSSION** To understand Nicolas's cunning plan, talk about the following questions in pairs:

- What is astrology?
- How do we know that Jean-Pierre believes in it?
- What kinds of predictions do astrologers make?
- What was Noah's flood (check with the footnote on page 65)?
- What exactly does Jean-Pierre think is going to happen, and how does he plan to save himself?

**ARTWORK** Draw a sketch of the set to show the three tubs hanging from the rafters and Nicolas's bedroom. (Don't show the characters.) So that the rest of the play can work, the bedroom should (a) be about two metres off the ground; and (b) have a small window. Save the sketch so that you can add to it in a moment.

*Accordion music indicates the entrance of a new character: ABSALON. This is also the cue for the other PILGRIMS to leave, as surreptitiously as possible.*

Ah, what I haven't told you yet is that Nicolas isn't the only bloke with designs on the carpenter's wife. Down the road lives Absalon, a young vicar, and 'e's been trying to get off with her for months. Finally 'e's plucked up the courage. But some people have a knack of picking the wrong moment...

*ABSALON has entered, a young padré. He puts a ladder up to ALISON's window and calls out.*

ABSALON      Alice! Alice, it is me, my sweet!

NICOLAS      *(To ALICE.)* 'Oo is it?

ALICE      Ah, it is Absalon. Always 'e pester me! Attend! I 'ave an idea!

*She draws the curtains across her window, so that we can no longer see her. Meanwhile ABSALON climbs the ladder.*

ABSALON      *(Calling through her window.)* Alice! I love you! Give me a kiss, my little cabbage, and make me a 'appy man!

*The curtains are pulled apart to reveal a joke-shop fake bum (representing Alice's). He kisses it loudly and long. Pauses. Thinks. Touches the bum. And nearly falls off his ladder in horror.*

I have kissed a bim! (*Hearing their laughter as the bum is swiftly withdrawn behind the curtain, Absalon grinds his teeth in fury.*) I must 'ave revenge! Honneur must be satisfied!

*He exits to more accordian music and returns, as the MILLER fills in the story…*                                                                    **90**

**MILLER**    So Absalon belts off to 'is mate, Gervase the blacksmith, borrows the 'ottest branding iron 'e can lay hands on, and makes his way straight back…

**ABSALON**    (*Having once again climbed the ladder.*) Alice! C'est moi! I 'ave a little present for you. Come to me again, my little clove of garlic!

*NICOLAS looks out of another window and whispers to ALICE:*

**NICOLAS**    Mais non! Ziz time eet is mah turn!

*The curtains whip open to reveal another rump, rather bigger than the first. As ABSALON approaches, he cunningly checks on its exact* **100** *whereabouts:*

**ABSALON**    Speak to me, my little sparrow.

*The bottom lets rip a terrifically rude noise – a trombone rendition of 'La Marseilleise' – and its cheeks vibrate in time to it. ABSALON thrusts home with the iron; the bottom disappears, NICOLAS screams and shouts 'Water! Water!'; the CARPENTER wakes, hears the cries and calls, 'Water? Ze flood 'as begun!', cuts the rope*

**C'est moi** *it's me.*

**Mais non!** *Oh, no!*

**La Marseilleise** *the French national anthem.*

*supporting his tub and plummets to the ground. As ALICE draws the curtains to reveal NICOLAS sitting in a chamber pot with steam rising round his bare haunches, music brings the tale to an end and accompanies the MILLER's brief epilogue...*

**MILLER**
So Nick and Alice got their oats,
The carpenter was thwarted.
And Absalon has kissed her bum –
The perfect ending! Sorted!

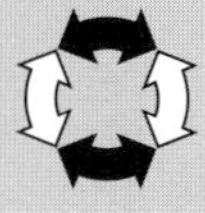

**ARTWORK AND FREEZE-FRAMING** Add characters to the sketch of the set you produced earlier (see page 66) to show your favourite moment from the end of the tale. Then, in small groups, freeze-frame the moment and compare your freeze-frame with other groups'.

*The cheering PILGRIMS are quietened by the HOST.*

**HOST**
All right! Well, we haven't heard all the tales by any means, but I suppose you could say that we've got through the first round. So what do you say we take a vote on the ones we've heard so far? Just to see who's in the lead.

*Receiving general approval for this idea, he continues.*

So let's just have a quick reminder. Day one of the pilgrimage we had...

*As the PILGRIMS cheer and applaud each title, it is clear that some of the tales have been enjoyed by some of the listeners more than others.*

**PARDONER**
...the story of the three crooks who go in search of Death...

**HOST**
...and on day two...

**REEVE**
...the tale of the stupid, drunken thieving miller, the creep...

**HOST**
Yes, thank you, Oswald.

**CHAUCER**
...on day three, my own small offering about the heroic Sir Topaze...

| | |
|---|---|
| **FRANKLIN** | …day four, the story of the soldier, the wife, the lover and the magician… |
| **MILLER** | …and day five: the Miller's Tale! Yes! |

*The HOST turns to face us, the theatre audience.*

**HOST**    Well? We've a couple of miles to Canterbury – taking it steady, we ought to get in another tale or two before we arrive. Quite a few more while we're there and half a dozen on the way back. That's one each, not four, as we'd originally planned, but, to be honest, I always thought that was a bit optimistic. Seems that Mr Chaucer's been writing them down. Hardly worth the effort, I'd have thought, but that's up to him. At least it means you can read up the ones you've missed. *(Turning back to the PILGRIMS.)* Right, then! Who's in the lead after round one? Hands up for…   **140**

*But, before we can find out the pilgrims' favourite tale so far, music drowns out the HOST's words and the lights dim.*

# THE END

**ARTWORK** Complete the map you started on page 45, adding details of the remaining days, inns and tales.

**WRITING AND DISCUSSION** Draw up four columns. In the first, list the tales; in the second, write a brief summary of what happened in each tale; in the third, give each tale a position to show where you would place it (1st for the one you liked most, down to 5th); in the fourth column, next to '1st', write down three reasons for choosing that tale as your favourite. Hold a class discussion to see which tale received the most 'firsts' and to compare the reasons for your choices.

**WRITING** Write two postcards from Canterbury from two very different pilgrims (such as the Prioress and the Miller). Each one should include comments on what they have liked and disliked about the pilgrimage so far. Try to write in styles that will match the characters' personalities.

# Looking back at the play

**1   Discussion: casting the roles**
In pairs, discuss which film or television actors you would cast in each of the following roles, noting down brief reasons to support your choices: the Host; Chaucer; the Miller; the Cook; the Wife of Bath; the Pardoner; and any other pilgrims or characters from the tales that you find particularly interesting. Compare your ideas in a class discussion.

**2   Artwork and writing: designing a poster**
Work in pairs to design a poster advertising a stage, television or film version of *The Canterbury Tales*. First discuss as a class the words and images that usually appear on a poster of this kind. Try to bring out the fact that each of the tales is set in a different period.

**3   Artwork and writing: a theatre programme**
Create a programme for a theatre performance of *The Canterbury Tales*. Remember to include a cast that you have decided on, as well as any illustrations that would be helpful to the audience.

**4   Discussion and writing: a review**
In small groups, talk about which of the tales you enjoyed most: the Pardoner's, the Reeve's, Chaucer's, the Franklin's or the Miller's. Which one was voted top by your class?

For each tale, discuss features such as the plot, the characters, the dialogue, the setting, and the level of excitement, mystery or humour. Then, on your own, write a review of the tale you considered to be the best.

**5   Writing: a moral tale**
Write a story or a play which (a) has a 'moral', or message; or (b) which poses a question for us to think about. (For example, the Pardoner's Tale seems to have messages about greed and death; the Franklin's Tale asks us to think about the right way to behave and how we should treat one another.)

**6    Discussion and writing: ten years on**

Discuss what each of the following might be doing ten years after the end
of the pilgrimage: the Host; the Wife of Bath; the Miller; or a character of
your choice. Then write a letter from the pilgrim to a friend, explaining how
the pilgrimage of ten years earlier changed them.

**7    Writing: a radio play**

Some of the tales could work very well on radio (the Reeve's, for obvious
reasons, would not). Select one of the tales and (i) list the sound effects
and music which might be required; and (ii) redraft a section of the tale as a
radio script.

**8    Artwork: creating a display**

Create a classroom display to represent the tales and the pilgrims. You
could include:

- Brief summaries of the five tales;
- Drawings and descriptions of the pilgrims;
- Artwork, such as: storyboard frames, designs for staging and costume,
  newspaper reports, timelines, drawings of characters and key props;
- The posters and theatre programmes created for activities 2 and 3
  above.

**9    Reseach: life in Chaucer's England**

The pilgrims in this play and the tales they tell are based on characters and
stories in a long narrative poem by Geoffrey Chaucer written towards the
end of the 1300s. In pairs, look back through the play, and the activities you
have completed, and note down everything you have learned about
Chaucer's world. You could make notes under the following headings:

- trades and professions;
- religion and the church;
- ideas and stories;
- inns and travel.

It will also help to reread the introduction on page VI. When you have
completed your notes, write a page for a school history book on 'Life in
Chaucer's England'.

**10  Language study**

Here is a section from the Pardoner's Tale as Chaucer wrote it. (We now call his language Middle English.) In pairs, (i) use the notes to work out a translation (don't write it in verse, like Chaucer's – try to make it as fluent as you can); and then (ii) decide which part of the story it comes from:

| | |
|---|---|
| For <u>right as</u> they hadde <u>cast</u> his deeth befoore, | *just as; planned* |
| <u>Right so</u> they han hym <u>slayn</u>, and that <u>anon</u>. | *in exactly that way;* |
| | *killed; straightaway* |
| And whan that this was <u>doon</u>, thus spak that <u>oon</u>: | *done; one of them* |
| "Now lat us sitte and drynke, and make us merie, | |
| And afterward we <u>wol</u> his body berie." | *will* |
| And with that word <u>it happed hym, par cas</u>, | *he happened by chance* |
| To take the <u>botel</u> <u>ther</u> the poyson was, | *bottle; in which* |
| And drank, and <u>yaf</u> his <u>felawe</u> drynke also, | *gave; fellow (friend)* |
| For which anon they <u>storven</u> bothe two. | *died* |

**11  Discussion**

When Chaucer wrote *The Canterbury Tales* in the fourteenth century, he did not set each tale in a different historical period, as this play version does. In pairs, talk about what is added by giving each tale its own setting:

- The Pardoner's: 1950s crooks;
- The Reeve's: 1920s silent movie;
- Chaucer's: mid-twentieth-century cricket match;
- The Franklin's: nineteenth-century India when it was part of the British Empire;
- The Miller's: comic-book French farce.